The Autism Mom's Survival Guide

ALSO BY SUSAN SENATOR

Making Peace with Autism

THE

Autism Mom's

Survival

Guide ^(for dads, too!)

Creating a Balanced and Happy Life
While Raising a Child with Autism

Susan Senator

TRUMPETER
Boston & London
2010

Some names have been changed to protect individuals' privacy.

Trumpeter Books
An imprint of Shambhala Publications, Inc.
Horticultural Hall
300 Massachusetts Avenue
Boston, Massachusetts 02115
www.shambhala.com

9 8 7 6 5 4 3 2 1

First edition
Printed in Canada

♾ This edition is printed on acid-free paper that meets the
American National Standards Institute z39.48 Standard.
♻ This book was printed on 100% postconsumer recycled
paper. For more information please visit www.shambhala.com.

Distributed in the United States by Random House, Inc.,
and in Canada by Random House of Canada Ltd

Interior design and composition: Greta D. Sibley & Associates

Library of Congress Cataloging-in-Publication Data
Senator, Susan.
The autism mom's survival guide (for dads, too!): creating a balanced and
happy life while raising a child with autism / Susan Senator.
  p.   cm.
Includes index.
ISBN 978-1-59030-753-3 (pbk.: alk. paper)
1. Parents of autistic children. 2. Autistic children—Care. I. Title.
RJ506.A9.S456 2010
649'.154—dc22
2009034557

This book is dedicated to all autism families,
especially to those who so graciously invited me
into their homes and lives. I loved meeting all of you
and listening to your stories, your wonderful voices, and
meeting your kids. All of you helped me make sense of
the autism parenting experience, and showed me
a thing or two about what is important in life.

Contents

Preface

IS BEING AN AUTISM PARENT fundamentally different from parenting other types of children? It's hard to say. Most parents go through challenges with their children and grapple with uncertainty about their kids' development and how best to help them through their struggles. But we do know that autism parents *perceive* themselves to be up against more than most parents, and that perception itself is tremendously significant because it can make raising a child with autism feel unnecessarily terrible and hopeless.

Having a child on the autism spectrum can bring many hardships, no question. But in terms of the parenting experience, how much of the struggle—how much of the grief, depression, and despair—is caused by our children's actual impairments, and how much is due to our own level of misinformation and confusion, the lack of adequate help and support, the cultural stigma surrounding autism, and the resulting inability to nurture ourselves adequately?

My son Nat was diagnosed with autism at age three, and his disabilities are relatively severe. However, over my twenty years as Nat's mother, I have come to believe that it's not the autism itself that has caused us the most suffering but our perceptions of it, our mental and emotional "baggage" surrounding autism, that has had the biggest negative impact on our lives. Following the publication of my first book, *Making Peace with Autism,* I gave talks around the United States, and I learned that many autism parents have come to the same conclusion: the perception, confusion, and ignorance surrounding autism are equal to, if not more problematic than, autism itself.

This book is written with this realization in mind. It focuses on those debilitating mental and emotional perceptions; it illustrates our experience as autism parents and attempts to clarify painful misconceptions we may have about our children and ourselves. My belief is that once we become aware of the negative ways we look at autism, things begin to open up for us: we start to gain valuable perspective, which is the autism parent's foundation for hope and, ultimately, happiness.

But how does that evolution come about for people?

I spent three years trying to find out. I collected the stories, discoveries, and hard-earned wisdom of autism parents in this country and abroad. I listened to these parents to try to understand all the things that they went through that allowed them, slowly, to gain perspective on autism, from the small tips and strategies to the major philosophical shifts. There are many aspects to happiness, to finding sanity, or not losing your way, that came into focus as I interviewed people. The parents I spoke with sugarcoated nothing. They gave me their stories and their trust, and I've tried to do justice to their words and thoughts. This book is dedicated to them and to all autism parents. May all of us find our well-deserved happiness.

Acknowledgments

THERE ARE A FEW INDIVIDUALS I want to acknowledge for helping in various ways to bring this book into being. My parents, who will read anything I write and like it. My sister Laura, who really gets it, and always has. My friends— Ruth, Emily, Sheila, Cynthia—who cheered me on or took me to coffee or lunch for the least little excuse. Hannah, who made five at the dinner table again when I so sorely needed it. Diane who goes above and beyond the definition of "agent," and stood by me when I was flipping out about how hard this project was. Eden, the most patient editor in the world. And Shambhala, a unique publishing house that is as idealistic and lovely as the works they produce.

And then, there is my family. My children: Max, the most graceful teenager I know, who sometimes hung out with me while I worked and showed me funny things on the Internet. Ben, who made me laugh, and Nat, for being my muse. And of course, Ned, the love of my life, who once said, "You want to be a writer? So write."

1

It's All How You Look at It
The Gift of Perspective

*A happy life consists not in the absence, but
in the mastery of hardships.*

—Helen Keller, "The Simplest Way to Be Happy"

WHEN MY SON Nat was diagnosed with autism at the age of
three, I had no idea how much autism was going to force me
to change: how I parented, how I made plans, who I hung out
with, how I felt about family, how I felt about my life. Those
changes were huge and fraught with emotion and intensity.
We didn't know what to tackle first—finding him a school
program, educating ourselves, finding specialists for him and
for us—but we realized fairly quickly that we had to do all of
these at once.

"How can I bear it?" I wrote in my journal a few months
after diagnosis. "Nat is being called a 'special ed' kid, the very
thing I dreaded. If I let everyone else decide that is what he is,
I feel like I'm giving up on him. I see myself as his last hope."

Back then I thought that if I accepted his diagnosis, it would make Nat's condition worse. I feared that it would change how we all saw him and treated him, in a way that would be harmful to him. This may have been magical thinking, but it is what I felt at the time.

I eventually realized that I had to let go of the old idea of him, of the prediagnosis innocence, and the visions I had of him that never really matched who he was. I also had to physically let him go, to release him from my protective embrace and into the guidance of a school where he could learn from others who could help him better than I could. And yet at the same time, I had to learn the best educational approaches, the most effective therapies, the day-to-day management of behaviors and communication issues. What's more, I had to learn about balancing all that Nat needed with my other children's needs, my marriage, and my own life—a tremendously difficult proposition. However, through years and years of parenting Nat (he's twenty years old as of this writing), I've come to see that all of this is possible—though not easy, and never perfect.

The most important thing I have realized in all this time is that autism is not tragic, it is not the end of things. I even knew this at times back in the early days, in fleeting moments of clarity when he was newly diagnosed. One day I wrote, "I know it's going to be OK. It already is. Whatever Nat is, he's alive, healthy, and wonderful." Of course this sweet ease that I felt in that moment did not last, but it did return, increasingly, over time.

Learning about a child's autism is an unfolding process. We

get to know that child through the particular filter of autism, but in doing so, we start to see him clearly and wholly. And that perspective is the beginning of our peace and progress.

How do we get to the blessed point where we finally step back and understand deeply that our children are whole, not broken? And that our own lives, by extension, are also whole and full of potential? In talking to parents, I learned that achieving this knowledge has nothing to do with our age, our child's age, or the severity of our child's problems; nor does it have to do with income, race, or any other factors we usually think of. For me, it took years, and then suddenly, things snapped into place one afternoon when Nat was thirteen, and we shared a single moment of connection—the last thing I would have expected at that time. In those days he would have long bouts of fake laughing, and I was just sick of it. On that particular afternoon I think I was just about to lose it when, probably punchy from emotional exhaustion and irritation, I just started laughing loudly right back at him. I kind of turned it into a teasing, mocking game, saying, "what's so funny, huh?" and poking him. Just acting, without thinking, with no hope for anything except an end to his annoying fake laughter.

But he loved it! He smiled and he looked at me with interest. His laughter—and mine—became warm and genuine. I realized then that he *wanted* me to laugh with him, to play with him; that he wanted to connect with me as much as I wanted to with him. That exchange was a pivotal moment in our relationship.

For other parents, achieving a sense of peace around an autistic child's struggles may happen early on—sometimes even when things are at their worst. One such parent I talked to, Kathleen, experienced a new clarity about her little son soon after helplessly enduring a nightmarish, epic tantrum. Kathleen, who lives in rural Maine with her two sons, Sammy and Oscar (two years apart, both on the autism spectrum), says that in the beginning she got little information and support from her healthcare providers. "I had no idea about therapies like Applied Behavior Analysis, nutritional supplements, or other therapies. We were just given a handshake and told, 'Good luck!'"

Though both children were on the spectrum, Oscar had more difficulties. One day the family reached a crisis point. "One afternoon, we went to the store," Kathleen explains, "and Oscar saw Little Bear toothpaste. I didn't see it, so I didn't buy it. At home that night, all of a sudden, he had to have it. He kept asking us where it was. In his mind, it was somewhere in the house and we weren't giving it to him. He just went out of his mind, slamming his head into the washing machine. There was nothing that I could say that would make him understand that we didn't have it. His tantrum went on for eight hours."

Kathleen says, "It just felt hopeless. I sat there looking at him and there was nothing I could do or say to help him calm down. I loved him and yet I also hated him—and I felt horrible for hating him. There he was, all of four and a half years old, and in my head I was wishing him away. I locked myself in the bathroom and just cried."

Finally Oscar exhausted himself and she was able to hold him and rock him into a good place. "That night my husband and I held each other for many hours," she says. "It was the first time that we felt there was no hope, like this was forever. This was a turning point. I realized that with my older son we'd just done things by the seat of our pants. But this approach wasn't working for Oscar—and we couldn't go on like this."

The next day Kathleen started asking for help, which she says is still very hard for her. "I've always been an independent person. But I started asking other parents for ideas." Kathleen found a new neurologist, who put Oscar on medication. "The public perception is that we overmedicate our kids because their behavior is inconvenient," she says. "I felt terrible guilt about putting him on medication, but something had to change—we just couldn't survive the way things were."

For Oscar, the meds worked phenomenally well. "On medication, he was able to just be," says Kathleen. "Zoloft stopped his repetitive cycles of hell (his obsessive-compulsive rituals). He could sit, he could play, and he could look at people."

Around this time, she says that she began to see Oscar as a separate person for the first time. "I had this realization: this has nothing to do with me, and I'm not in charge here! It's OK for me to admit that this really sucks. It's not his fault and it's not my fault."

"There is no right or wrong here," Kathleen realized. "I'm doing the best I can and then some." She says that, paradoxically, by acknowledging her powerlessness, she gained power. She also says that this was "the beginning of him," meaning that this terrible experience, followed by the realization that her son needed help beyond what she had been giving him, led her out of her old way of seeing Oscar. She was finally able to let go of her sense of failure and shame and focus on him. This experience caused her to seek help for him, to do the work she needed to do as his mother, rather than being incapacitated by helplessness.

In my own journey with autism, when I understood that my parenting ability was not the problem so much as my perceptions and misconceptions of Nat and autism, I could finally move forward. I think that on some level, Kathleen and I, like many autism moms, started out viewing our sons as "broken" or defective, and we saw ourselves as being at fault. That was very counterproductive. Although certainly I did have my hands full—a whole universe of challenge and learning ahead of me because Nat's autism was so different from anything I had ever encountered before—not being able to fix him created a feeling of shame around Nat and made everything that was difficult about being Nat's mother that much worse.

In time I learned to see autism as something that shaped a lot of Nat's actions, but not *him*. Autism was one context for our family life, but not the entirety of it; therefore it was not a threat to our family's happiness. Or, as Kathleen put it, as something "that was not all of my child, but only a part of my child." Our perspective on this disorder makes all the difference. I truly believe that none of us can be happy until we understand that. For me, understanding that has taken a lot of difficult trips to the playground, a lot of cups of coffee with friends, and a lot of therapy. Now I know that I am not alone in my experience of isolation and feeling overwhelmed, related in some ways only, I now see, to my child's autism.

The perception of autism has always been devastatingly negative, from Bruno Bettelheim's theory that autism is caused by the "Refrigerator Mother" (a mother who is cold and unresponsive to her child), to Michael Savage, the radio talk show host, and his rant about autism just being about spoiled kids and lousy parents, to the most recent offense, comedian Denis Leary, who wrote in his book, *Why We Suck*:

> *There is a huge boom in autism right now because inattentive mothers and competitive dads want an explanation for why their dumb-ass kids can't compete academically, so they throw money into the happy laps of shrinks . . . to get back diagnoses that help explain away the deficiencies of their junior morons. I don't [care] what these crackerjack whack jobs tell you—your kid is not autistic. He's just stupid. Or lazy. Or both.*

Later on, Leary said that the quote was taken out of context, and he apologized to parents whom he had offended. And yet, for some autism parents, Leary's words stung because they summed up their own irrational fears that they are terrible parents with terrible kids. The quote was a lightning rod for a societal attitude that autism is a defect in the child or the parent, rather than a disability with its own particular issues in need of accommodation and understanding. It seems as if autism-parent bashing is always with us in one form or another.

In addition to the negative perceptions and stereotypes, autism parents must also cope with the tangled and confusing web of theories, treatments, and information about autism. Even though living with autism is often very difficult, there is no need to get stuck on that. The story need not end there, the focus need not be on the difficult and negative. Parents can seek ways to be happier. Parents can still lead worthwhile lives and find happiness with their children and on their own.

In Nat's early days, my feelings were a chaotic mess. Often I felt ashamed of him because he was so different from the children around him. At the beginning of Nat's third year I wrote, "I'm so unhappy I feel like dying. I feel so hopeless, so stagnant. Three-year-olds grow up, get toilet-trained. Not mine. He is as out of it as last year this time. He won't talk to me. He won't answer anyone. He won't play with kids. I can't help him. I feel like I failed."

In those days I was filled with fear, dread, and despair because I did not really know what autism meant—or what it would mean to us. I worried that the diagnosis was a confirmation of my defects as a parent and a person. How could it not be? My images of autism at that time were formed out of ignorance: Dustin Hoffman as the bizarre, fairly helpless character in the movie *Rain Man,* or portrayals of children banging their heads, out of control. This autism could only be a bad thing.

Other times, though, I saw that Nat was *not* the problem, but in some way *I* was. I was in my late twenties and struggling with so many things, depression most prominently. Becoming Nat's mother forced me to deal with my old stuff, to focus on myself and become a real, strong adult. From their first days of life, our children challenge us to rise to our fullest potential. In the end, they teach us acceptance of limitations, acceptance of what is.

In the early days, nothing in my life remained clear. Or when I did reach some understanding of Nat or autism, it would just as quickly disappear, because he would change again. I thought that this was unique to me, but with years of therapy (and growing up) I finally understood that all parents feel that way. What's more, no one has the perfect life. I also had to learn that although autism was a big, difficult, and defining configuration in my life, it was not *the* definition (and for that matter, neither was autism the definition of all that Nat was).

Looking at how my own understanding of autism has evolved, and at the journeys of other parents, I realize that it is no wonder we parents have such a terrible time dealing with autism in the early years. From the beginning, my understanding of autism was skewed. I thought that it meant Nat was some kind of mysterious creature, a wild child. I also worried that I had caused his autism, and I was terrified by what others would think and how they would treat him. Doctors, teachers, neighbors, grandparents, and many people around us, including we ourselves, carry around what I call disability baggage—all kinds of biases and misconceptions we might not even be aware of—and it can often make a difficult situation worse.

How many of us autism parents have been faulted, or felt at fault, for our children's struggles? In the early days I was terrified that Nat's issues were my doing. Somehow, somewhere, had I rejected him or had I been unable to love him? The reality was, I was so afraid of my new responsibility with this first baby of mine, and so unformed myself, that I was usually in a horrible state. My love for this vulnerable, quiet baby was fierce and actually scared me. Every emotion around Nat was so mixed, so intense. Nothing was straightforward.

So often the anguish of autism parents is born of this kind of confusion and misunderstanding: the problem lies more in what we do to ourselves *much more than anything our child does.* Autism mothers have so much uncertainty about the origins of their child's distress and difficulties, and that may be the real root of our struggles. Despite all the current information about this disorder, autism parents often worry that they somehow are at fault. Combine that emotional state with the horrible image of autism you see everywhere, and you have a very heavy burden that only gets in the way of parenting your autistic child.

There is nothing I want more than to relive those early days "right"—and by "right" I mean enjoying Nat just as he was.

I wish that I had known enough to get him into Early Intervention, to start him in some kind of hard-core intensive preschool to boost his development and skills. But so much more than that, I wish that *I* had been OK: I wish that I had already done my growing up and my own psychological healing *before* I became his mother. I wish I could have been whole enough to embrace every Nat-ism, to be proud of his differences, and to accept his unique, atypical development and way of doing things. I think a lot of autism parents come to feel that way.

AUTISM AND MATERNAL DEPRESSION

Dr. Marion O'Brien, professor of human development and family studies at the University of North Carolina, has studied autism mothers and the challenges they face. Though she began studying the mothers of special-needs children in general, she found such a prevalence of depressive symptoms in autism mothers that she shifted the focus of her study to autism mothers. Dr. O'Brien studied close to seventy families and found a high incidence of depressive symptoms among the mothers, a condition she attributed to the phenomenon of "ambiguous loss," whereby a parent, mothers in particular, feel a massive, shapeless grief about their child's disorder.

While many psychologists and therapists attribute this depression to a phase of the grieving process, Dr. O'Brien concluded from her studies that the autism mothers' depression was not "as clear-cut as a grief process" because the child has not passed away. "You still have a child," she says. "But he or she is not the child you thought or hoped you had." The strongest recommendation that came out of Dr. O'Brien's study was for depressed autism mothers to seek treatment, to take care of themselves *rather than waiting for something to change in their children*. The wisdom I took away from this study was to find ways to be happy—and to get professional help if necessary—regardless of the disability or other challenges in your family.

Another study, published by the American Academy of Pediatrics, found that there is nearly twice the incidence of depression and other psychiatric disorders in autism parents than in the general population.* These findings are depressing in and of themselves, making me wonder about the effects this kind of information could have on autism parents. Although certainly research like this is important, we autism parents are exposed to so much negative information about autism as it is that I wonder how much this sort of data really helps us. Regardless, it's clear that we need to find ways to help ourselves so that we don't get sucked into depression and hopelessness, either from our families' actual challenges or from the bleak aura surrounding autism information.

For many autism families, the early years before and after diagnosis are traumatic and affect our outlook going forward. The negative beginnings with one's child can be difficult to let go of and can make it difficult to develop a healthy, balanced lifestyle later on. Many autism parents get trapped in cycles of self-recrimination. Whatever else we must deal with—getting our child the right therapies, a good school program, help in the home—so many autism parents have always had the double whammy of self-doubt and judgment from others. Is it any wonder so many of us feel depressed?

---

*Julie Daniels et al., "Parental Psychiatric Disorders Associated with Autism Spectrum Disorders in the Offspring," *Pediatrics* 121, no. 5 (May 2008): http://pediatrics.aappublications.org/cgi/reprint/121/5/e1357.pdf.

If, however, your earliest experience with autism is not very negative, you may be able to have a more optimistic, accepting view of your child—and yourself—from the beginning. Lisa from New Jersey is one mom I spoke to who feels that because of the particular diagnosis her child was given, she was allowed to feel quite hopeful for a long time. Lisa now believes that her child received a milder diagnosis than he should have (he was initially considered to have low-functioning Asperger's), but this diagnosis allowed her to see him as being less impaired and helped her focus simply on what he needed, rather than getting lost in despair.

"At four years old there was a lot of hope for my son," she says. She still maintains her sense of hope, though. "He's still young, only nine years old. On the other hand, maybe we're still in denial." Lisa does worry that this is going to be a life-long trial. She has friends around her who "don't have hope, who think only about how autism is a lifelong thing."

On the other hand, some parents actually feel liberated and positive right away, just knowing what it is that they are dealing with. Carolyn, a mom from Maryland, explained to me how she manages to view her son's autism in a positive light. "It was very simple," she said. "It wasn't cancer." This response shocked me a little, until she told me the rest. "Four months after my only son was diagnosed with autism, one of his friends was diagnosed with Stage 4 cancer at the age of three and a half. When I called my husband, who was on a business trip, to tell him about my friend's little boy, he said, 'Thank God our child just has autism!'" Watching this beloved child and his parents go through chemotherapy and surgeries has made her appreciate her situation. "What they have been through this year has made my experiences with autism pale in comparison," she says.

Carolyn also made a deep bond with this child's mother: "In some ways we have a lot in common. We're both mothers of only sons with husbands that often have to work long hours, and we're left alone to deal with our cranky boys a lot of the time. We've also had our dreams of a carefree parenthood stolen from us." For Carolyn, the shared experience with the other mom and her husband's attitude have helped her to gain perspective on autism relatively quickly.

In my case, the loving support of my husband helped me a great deal. When Ned and I drove home from that very first evaluation with Nat buckled into the backseat, I wondered what it meant that he had autism. What were the first and second steps? How would I tell people? Ned answered, very reasonably, "Maybe we don't tell people just yet." It hadn't occurred to me to let myself process all this information privately, at my own pace. Ned reminded me that this news, as difficult as it was, was indeed ours. And I was not alone. We were in it together. The power of at least one supportive person in an autism parent's life cannot be underestimated.

Another question that arose for me in the early days of diagnosis was: how was Nat different today than yesterday? We now knew the name of what we were dealing with. When we have a name for something that has confused and troubled us, we feel powerful, in control. But in reality, we knew nothing but fear and ignorance. Learning the name of something can sometimes give it more importance than need be, especially if you are not yet fully knowledgeable. Labeling can also help you face something—but it may be that you are facing it from a position of complete ignorance. Therefore, the ability to focus on our children themselves, on helping them, rather than becoming paralyzed by preconceived and uninformed notions, can be a tremendous positive factor in our early attitudes toward autism.

I am grateful, looking back, that our doctor pushed me toward the question "now what?"—that is, pushed me in the direction of taking action instead of spending too much time obsessing over the diagnosis. He also refrained from conjecture about Nat's future disability, and also avoided depressing me with what to expect or not expect from Nat's autism. Ultimately, what we needed to do was to discover who Nat really was—what aspects of his behavior were just him (essential and unchangeable) and in what ways he could be helped to grow and develop.

The two tasks—understanding who Nat is and knowing what to do for him—have been a lifelong mission (just like dealing with who *I* really am and what to do for me). I see parenting as a process of identifying what our children are struggling with and then figuring out how much of that is just *them,* who they are, and how much is something to fix. How much to accept, how much to change? Once we have the right balance, we can help the child and help ourselves live more worthwhile lives. I think that we autism parents first learn how to do this through parenting our children, and then parenting ourselves.

COPING WITH JUDGMENT
AND CRITICISM

Although Nat's diagnosis provided me with an answer, it opened a whole new chapter about dealing with the reality of disability. I wore my new knowledge with hostility, imagining everyone was judging me, and throwing my heartbreaking news into people's faces like a glass of ice water. I remember showing up at the playground with Nat and joining the women in my playgroup, who were sitting on the granite curb surrounding the sandbox. I didn't say much while they talked about the things they always talked about, such as cloth versus disposable diapers, favorite children's clothing catalogs, and feeding problems. But suddenly I blurted out something like, "They think Nat has autism." I remember my voice being hoarse, as if I could barely breathe the words. None of the moms said anything. I felt horrible, because I interpreted their silence to mean I was no longer welcome. "They are not my real friends," I wrote in my journal soon after. Looking back, I'm sure that is not what they were feeling about me and my news; most likely they were just uncertain about how to respond. Probably a hug would have been great, but all I got was awkward silence. The bitterness I felt—whether from their behavior or from my own feelings about autism—caused me to drop out of the playgroup.

Susan from Massachusetts says, "All I need from family and friends is for them to say something like, 'You are doing a great job.' Please don't blame me that my child is not cured!" It's not only the ignorance and judgment of others that makes our early days of diagnosis so difficult; parents also often feel judged by the vocal multitudes of autism parents who follow this or that regimen (more on this in chapter 2). In the end, all the vehemence and even desperation of other autism parents can end up making us simply despair rather than take appropriate action for our child or for ourselves. The judgments of others is a particularly difficult aspect of unhappiness in the autism parent.

And yet, at the same time, other autism parents can be an essential support. Soon after I left my playgroup, I sought out an autism support group, run by a local ARC (the named originally stood for "Association for Retarded Citizens" but is now known simply as the ARC). This group, made up of parents who were, for the most part, as confused and overwhelmed as me, was a lifesaver. Mothers I met there, along with others I've met through the Special Olympics, are my supports, my information resources, my confidantes, and my armor.

Many parents I talk to have felt saved by the encouragement and hope that their fellow school parents, local autism community groups, friends or family, Internet groups, or favorite blogs have given them. But there can also be a downside to support groups. In my earliest days of going to a support group, sometimes I could not stand being there because one particular father only talked about how well his twin girls were doing. The father crowed about how hard he worked, setting up all kinds of programs within their home to force the girls out of their private worlds and into productive play. I wanted to kill him, or kill myself. I thought I was working hard for Nat; why didn't he improve like these girls? Why did he still hardly ever talk? Why did my friend's kid, who seemed to be worse off than Nat at the beginning because he never talked, eventually lose most of his autism diagnosis and become fairly independent as a teen? Every time someone else's kid made progress, I would be outwardly happy for them, of course, but there was a part of me that was so angry, so jealous. Eventually I could not participate in support groups because everyone seemed to be competing for the award for "Most High-Functioning Kid" or playing the game "Whose Kid Can Pass as a Typical Kid?"

As we'll see in the next chapter, with the prevalence of very opinionated Internet groups, blogs, and advocacy organizations of every stripe springing up daily, parents can feel overwhelmed or even at fault for what they've done, not done, or believe. I have been lucky not to be openly criticized too often. But so many others I know have been. NancyBea told me, "I've had complete strangers tell me confidently that I could cure Henry if I just put him on a dairy-free diet."

Other parents encounter the same kind of hurtful messages. Raquel from Arizona has said, a number of times, "The autism community is not there to support your happiness. It's really about political agendas." Even though the autism community can be very supportive, a lifeline, it is just as true that the autism community can be its own worst enemy. I learned this again and again as an autism mother.

It is apparent that in order for us to help our children and ourselves, we are going to have to let go of our judgments—of ourselves and of others. Ultimately, such empathy will lead us to a greater understanding of autism, and with such understanding comes perspective, peace, and progress in our own lives as well as our children's.

We all have to learn how to help, accept, love, and parent this child as he is, in whatever mixture of autism and typical development he presents. Only then can we learn to find happiness with our children and with ourselves.

Though we face many struggles as autism parents, and though so much about our lives is not under our control, it is within our power to reduce a lot of the suffering we experience. We can do this by remembering to take care of ourselves, by figuring out how to have more fun with our kids, by nurturing our marriages, and, most important, by shifting our attitudes about autism.

Meanwhile, here's a list of ideas about how to get started shifting your attitude.

Freeing Yourself of the Autism Baggage

- Perhaps the first thing is to realize is that autism does not define your child and it does not have to define your family. The following article is helpful in understanding this concept: www.parents.com/baby/health/autism/dealing-with-autism/.

- The Autism Society of America (autism-society.org) is a good, accurate resource for many questions a parent might have about autism, and their approach is more inclusive of the views of autistic people than other large autism organizations. Their all-encompassing Web site goes to the best sources to learn about autism: autistics themselves and their parents.

- Understand that just as you have heard that each individual with autism has autism in their own unique way, you must remember *that each person with autism is a unique individual,* someone with particular gifts, quirks, talents, skills, emotions, and needs just like anyone else. It may take longer to know an autistic child or adult because *you will likely have problems communicating with each other,* but know that it is possible to communicate and connect, and therefore to *separate the person from what you may feel is negative about autism.*

- Look at the Web site of the late Dr. Bernard Rimland: autism.com. Most active in the 1960s, Rimland was one of the first medical professionals to see autism as a physiological, not a psychological, disorder. Rimland is also considered the father of biomedical treatment of autism. His Web site offers hope to parents who are actively seeking improvement in their children's skills using biomedical interventions.

- You may not be capable right now of distinguishing your child from the difficult behaviors that are associated with autism, but in time you will be. Give yourself time to evolve in your understanding of your child.

- Find comfort in positive accounts about living with autism, such as *Autism and the God Connection* by William Stillman, *George and Sam* by Charlotte Moore, and *Road Map to Holland* by Jennifer Graf Groneberg.

- Find your supports. Start a regular Mom's Night Out with kindred spirits. Get your venom out there, but confined to those you know. What happens in Mom's Night Out stays in Mom's Night Out.

- When interacting with other autism parents, make a vow to do no harm. Do not add to the Sturm und Drang around autism. All you need to do is to love and nurture your child, and perhaps help others. If you find you are being critical of other autism parents, take a step back and a deep breath, and stop it.

- Become aware of negative images of autism in the media that contribute to the "Autism is a monster" mentality. See the Autistic Self Advocacy Network (autisticadvocacy.org) for more information on these efforts.

- Start a positive Yahoo group or a blog. Spread the word about community building. Blogger.com is an easy and free blogging service. Creating Yahoo groups is simple. Go to groups.yahoo.com/. To spread the word about your group or your blog, put comments on other people's blogs so that they know where to find you. Also check out autismherd.blogspot.com as a good model for fun and positive autism blogs.

- If supports and resources are lacking in your community, try your hand at writing a letter to the editor of your local newspaper about this. Even if it doesn't get published, you'll feel like you've made an effort toward the good, and you will have clarified your feelings.

2

Surviving the Great Autism-Therapy Chase

AS AUTISM PARENTS, perhaps the biggest challenge to our happiness and peace of mind is our preoccupation with autism therapies. In my case, the question of which therapy or approach to try with Nat torments me as much as the disorder itself. Scientific research, education, and funding have not caught up with the high rate of diagnosis, so autism parents flounder around with a variety of approaches and strategies and depend on one another as much as on their doctors, specialists, and educators for guidance about which approaches to try. Autism care is done largely by feel, by trial-and-error more than anything else.

In autism treatment, it seems like the New Age meets the Dark Ages. On one hand there are a great deal of alternative treatments and philosophies, based not on science but on anecdote and intuition and which rely on dietary changes, oils, herbs, and vitamins. At the same time there are many autism treatments out there that seem bizarre or primitive, such as the unproven use of hyperbaric chambers, or the barbaric treatments like the aversive therapies that are still in use, which condone punishment such as electric shock therapy.

At every turn there are "experts" telling parents that they have just the right elixir or therapy to make their children well again, similar to the snake-oil salesmen of old. The promise of improvement, the hope of a brighter future for our children—this is the siren song that keeps all of us forever in thrall, forever wondering about what else, what more, we should be doing.

The history of Nat's therapies and educational approaches is a zigzag line that has never proceeded in an orderly, satisfying fashion. From the very beginning, we were told that there were no clear answers or protocols. But Ned and I were desperate to do something, so we focused on getting Nat into a beneficial school program, guided only by our doctor's very general, sphinxlike words: "No one can tell you which approach to choose, but you'll know when a program is working for him." Hearing this, we experienced, for the first time, but not the last, that burning, relentless need to get Nat the *right* treatment and not lose any time.

The first thing we did was find Nat a preschool run by a nearby public school system. Nat attended the program for nearly two years after his diagnosis, where he was included with many typically developing children, but he still was not communicating much, nor did his play skills evolve beyond twirling string in the sunlight. His teachers reported that he was "doing great" there, where he sat quietly during circle time without resistance and brought home lovely but suspiciously sophisticated artworks of glue and glitter. Was this really *Nat's* work? When the teachers explained to me their "hand-over-hand" technique, I was dismayed. Had Nat actually learned to create art in this fashion, or was it really the teacher's hands? It seemed far more likely that Nat was not truly learning art or other subjects; he was being led around like a puppet.

Nat was content in the program, but was this enough? Was this progress? I didn't think it was working. I knew I had to find him a more effective program. But I still did not know what "effective" would look like. There was always a cloud of uncertainty disturbing our equanimity, and perhaps affecting our judgment.

We moved Nat from school to school in a perpetual panic to get things exactly right for him, not knowing that this was possibly an unattainable goal. We thought of little else, even though we had two other children in our family. We eventually chose a private school that used behavioral techniques. Although its repetitious drilling and positive reinforcement (with candy, tickles, and praise) were at odds with our own free-and-easy parenting style, the caring and intensely animated teachers made the program very attractive. The school also trained me in the use of reward systems: M&Ms when Nat used the toilet or played pretend for a given length of time. Within a few months, we could see that this strategy was working in terms of gently leading him into a more diverse skill set, especially in the school environment. However, we were still dealing with Nat's passivity in most activities, particularly social and play, and his limited language. He would only echo our questions, rather than responding to them with his own answers. And sometimes he would still seem so lost, smiling or laughing charmingly to himself but never letting us in on the joke.

When we heard of a doctor who was having some success treating his autistic patients' social difficulties with Prozac and Zoloft (a class of antidepressants known as SSRIs), we thought that this might give Nat that extra boost. And indeed, after using Zoloft for about a year, Nat's language ability developed exponentially. By the time he was ten, he was occasionally expressing his desires and telling jokes. We were beside ourselves with joy. We wanted more. We thought that we had found the answer in the SSRIs.

We acted swiftly, moving him from his small classroom to a more academically challenging, mainstream type of classroom (with typically developing students and a regular curriculum). There were fewer supports there for him, but the director said to us, "Imagine the doors that would open if he could make it in this kind of program." And we agreed because we wanted more: we wanted a mainstreamed kid! What autism parent didn't dream of that? All we had to do was help him continue on this new trajectory, set into motion by the Zoloft.

We did not realize until it was too late that sometimes you don't get more by doing more.

Within months, Nat's behavior changed radically, perhaps

due to a higher dosage of Zoloft, or from the stress of the new classroom. Poor Nat became so destabilized that he became horribly aggressive and he was expelled. He was home for two months, where he became increasingly volatile, while we waited for a new placement. We hired a tutor for him, who stopped coming after Nat attacked her. It now seemed like we had lost everything.

Even now, when I think back, I don't truly understand what happened, but I feel so sad about it. It feels to me now like there had been a wave approaching, but our backs were turned away as we watched Nat progress, then were completely knocked over as Nat was swept away from us again.

In retrospect, Ned and I were guilty of the same mistake made by so many autism parents: pushing too hard, stretching our kid and everyone around him to the point of distortion. Did we do it out of love and hope? Of course. But did we also do it out of our own (human) vanity? Out of a sense of hubris? Probably.

Now that Nat is twenty, we know that effective treatments and school programs are only part of the picture of a successful, happy family. We know that the questions we need to ask are: Can Nat handle something new right now? What is best for Nat *and* for us? Now I know that if he can do more, competently and happily, than he could in a previous year, then he has progressed. In looking toward the future, my expectations should be based on where he is now and where he was a year ago, not on where he is now and where (or whom) I would like him to be. I should be able to see some positive changes in behavior management, in self-calming skills, in communication abilities, and in general self-care in the school setting and then hopefully generalized to other settings such as home and his workplace. Simple, and yet one of the most difficult things I have ever had to learn. My doctor was right, but then again, I could have used a lot more guidance than "you'll know when something's working." I wish my doctor had also said to me, "But remember that you also have to keep everything in your lives in balance. A peaceful family spirit is good therapy, too."

THE BURDEN OF "THE SPECTRUM"

The autism spectrum is large and varied. Many children are being diagnosed with some form of autism, and yet the distinctions between one type of autism and another are fuzzy at best. We might use the terms "low-functioning" or "high-functioning," but what does that mean exactly? Is "low-functioning" even a fair designation, when it derives its meaning mostly from a child's verbal abilities? Nat would be considered fairly low-functioning by this measure. He would be considered extremely delayed because of how he tests. And yet most people do not experience Nat that way at all. He is connected to us with his bright but evanescent smile and happy eyes. He helps with every single chore around the house, as competently and more willingly than his brothers. He is conscientious about doing most things we need him to do, clearing his place after meals, helping me with laundry, even making phone calls (albeit brief and labored) to grandparents. The list goes on. Very often the labels on the autism spectrum do not really fit the child, leaving parents in a quandary about many issues, from best treatments to prognosis.

The designation "low-functioning" or "severe" cannot possibly make anyone feel hopeful. Even more important, how do we know that autistics do not understand what is being said around them or about them? I have come to know many autistics from attending conferences and through e-mail and blogs, and I have learned that so many of them have been labeled one thing or another, and invariably the label does some kind of harm.

The labeling leads to confusion, too. There are so many people being called "autistic" who are so very different from one another, to the point that some people might dismiss some forms of autism as not being autism at all. Some people might feel that their child was misdiagnosed as "worse" than he ended up being, while others might observe the same kind of progress in their child and take all the credit for it because they feel they did so much to make their child "better."

There was complete agreement among those I interviewed that the haziness of the spectrum causes problems for families. There is definitely a need to break down the different presentations of autism and for scientists to decipher which forms of autism respond best to which therapies. Families need help determining whether their children actually improved due to whatever therapies they're using, or if they were simply misdiagnosed as "lower functioning" at the first office visit.

The biggest and most agonizing question among autism parents is this: If these children are all autistic, why do their outcomes vary so much? Why do some children seem to benefit from certain therapies while others do not? It is this confusion that gives autism a particularly soul-consuming quality for parents. Unlike most other medical diagnoses, there's little precision or clarity—about what the disorder is, what the prognosis is, or about how best to treat it.

Raquel from Arizona was spitting mad when I first talked to her about her child's autism. The ambiguity of the spectrum left her filled with a sense of frustration and impotence. She felt she was being led nowhere by doctors, autism books, and the autism community at large. "With most other special needs, you know more," Raquel said, and as the mother of both a child with cerebral palsy and one with autism, she should know. "With my older son, who has CP, we looked into a couple of alternative therapies. But we understood that no matter what, he's still going to have CP. We weren't going to be able to cure him." In the case of autism, however, many parents and professionals feel that one therapy or another can not only improve a child's functioning but can actually cure them.

Raquel, like many autism parents, believes that autism is a unique childhood disorder in that so many children are diagnosed but so little is known about best practice, treatment, and prognosis. "What we're calling autism is probably a bunch of different things," Raquel says. Although not everyone I talked to would agree with Raquel on this assertion, most parents would agree that the spectrum is huge and varied and that that in itself can be an obstacle to our peace of mind.

For one thing, autism parents don't know how drastically any particular child's condition can change over the years, and they also don't know *why* things change. "There are children who get 'better,'" Raquel agreed. "It doesn't happen to the majority of them, though. No one can really tell you *how* autistic your kid is." There are many stories of how a child was first diagnosed with something like PDD-NOS (Pervasive Developmental Disorder, Not Otherwise Specified) but now has the milder diagnosis of Asperger's. Or, as in Nat's case, we were first told he had "expressive language disorder with autistic-like symptoms," which then became PDD, and later just plain autism. What does it really mean, in the end, if parents do not know which path of treatment to follow, or what to expect for their children's progress?

Even those in the medical profession agree that "the spectrum" can be misleading and unwieldy for parents. Dr. Tim Buie, a pediatric gastroenterologist at Massachusetts General Hospital, is conducting groundbreaking research that explores the connection between digestive disorders and autistic symptoms. Buie told me that he believes the medical establishment is going to have to change how it deals with and thinks about autism. Understanding which kind of autism a child has, honing the diagnosis beyond pervasive developmental disorder, high-functioning autism, or Asperger's syndrome, may be the first step, with a unified research effort as the next. But it has to happen soon, Buie says: "There're one million people with autism. They need care now. They need better standards."

But the standards are a moving target. Because of the breadth of the spectrum, many parents feel confused or that the perception of their children's issues and challenges is inaccurate. "I think that there are many individuals on the autism spectrum who really do not have autism, but injuries from toxic exposure to their environment," wrote Jennie from Florida. "Maybe in thirty years the medical establishment will get enough studies together to realize there is an epidemic and give it a new name, such as 'toxic environment syndrome' or something. The autism spectrum is a wide range of disorders and it is so confusing to families to be given this diagnosis and no real guidance as to how to treat it, because each of our children are so different and respond to different interventions."

Adding to the anguish and stress that many autism parents feel is the slow growth of scientific research into causes and treatments. The science of autism has not kept pace with the increasing diagnosis of autism spectrum disorder (ASD). The number of therapies that abound, without clear guidelines or recommendations from the medical establishment, contribute in large part to the autism blame game and to unhappy parents. And finally, the resources that we all compete for—quality special ed programs, therapists, skills groups, adult services and supported living, and family supports—are much too scarce.

When parents first get the diagnosis, they generally head for the computer to see what the Internet says. Maybe they also find a local support group, but today it is more likely that they find e-mail lists or blogs that resonate with their intuition about their child. The e-mail groups and the blogs reinforce what the parent believes, and this is excellent support, even though it might not actually be accurate information or the best direction for the parent to go with the child.

If something happens whereby the child no longer responds to the approaches promulgated by the support group, then the parents may feel incompetent, angry, alienated, or all of the above. Parents then have to wade through new approaches, maybe checking with the pediatrician, but maybe not. Most likely they check with their autism friends and, of course, the Internet. It is very easy to find a group for nearly every approach, unfounded or unproven, and a practitioner willing to try this on one's child.

The difficulty of obtaining reliable expertise is as much a problem today as I found it to be nearly twenty years ago, except that now the problem is an overabundance of choices, with no clear markers as to whose advice to follow. Parents must be as well informed and discerning as possible, but where do they start?

"What does your doctor say?" my mother used to ask me of my former pediatrician, and it made me so frustrated. The *doctor*!? Our pediatrician at that time knew less than me! She hadn't even noticed that Nat had developmental problems and needed to be evaluated for autism. I finally took Nat for an office visit, armed with a list of all the developmental milestones Nat had missed, and then she finally agreed with me that there might be a problem. This was when he was nearly three. All of the information we had on autism screamed, "Zero to three are the crucial years for intervention!" I had also read that the brain is most malleable before age five, so I felt hopeless. I thought that I had missed that boat. Nat did not even get into a good program until he was nearly six. What did that mean for him? If he had been diagnosed at eighteen months, would he be less disabled today? A part of me always wonders, but now I can choose to let go of this question—now that he is twenty years old (usually I can, except on a bad day).

Not knowing what protocol to follow causes legitimate anguish in autism parents. If you don't really understand what the diagnosis means for your child, or what treatment strategy is called for, how can you possibly help him? How can you and your entire family function peacefully and happily? While other acute disabilities also bring with them a certain degree of confusion, few have come into the public consciousness with this level of haziness and bewilderment, and even fewer are as new a diagnosis.

NancyBea from Philadelphia says she has been through many twists and turns and dead ends with her son because of the lack of hard scientific evidence and guidance from autism experts. "At times I feel like I'm living in a nightmare, like something out of Kafka," she says, describing her agonizing pursuit of autism treatments, all the different things she has tried for her autistic son, with little or no success in gaining valuable skills such as behavior management or verbal communication. Autism parents need better advice from their specialists to help them choose or reject new therapies.

What I want to draw attention to is the *effect* on many parents of the current state of autism diagnosis and treatment. The lack of trust in the autism community combined with the dearth of clear and consistent guidance from the medical professionals; the flood of conjecture and information about alternative therapies, cures, and treatments; and the fact that no one knows what to try, how much to try, or when to stop trying, all chip away at the autism parent's ability to nurture their children effectively and erode their own sense of happiness and well-being.

THE AUTISM DIVIDE

Within the autism community there's a fundamental division between those who believe there is a cure and those who do not. I refer to this split as "the autism divide." Most autism parents have found themselves on one side or the other, and the zealous defense of the beliefs of either side can be very intimidating and destructive.

In general, those in the cure camp tend to believe that autism is the result of an injury—one that can be corrected. These folks believe that perhaps the disability has been caused by a vaccine, mercury poisoning, or other harm to the body from toxins in the environment (lead or food additives, for example), and that autism is not necessarily permanent. In this view, if you implement a special diet (such as the gluten-free, casein-free, or GFCF, diet), or if you administer substances that draw out heavy metals such as lead or mercury (a process called chelation), you can either reduce the symptoms of autism or reverse it entirely. This use of diet, vitamin supplements, and/or chelation to control and ameliorate autistic symptoms is also known as "the biomedical approach."

The biomedical approach is one of the more popular schools of thought among parents these days. Two of the biggest advocates for biomedical treatment are DAN (Defeat Autism Now) and Generation Rescue. Both organizations are composed of doctors, parents, advocates, and therapists who recommend dietary and nutritional interventions to their autistic patients, sometimes after putting them through myriad medical tests. One of the reasons for these organizations' popularity—aside from perceived success—is that their philosophy makes intuitive sense to some people. Biomedical treatments also give the parent the feeling of hands-on control over their child and, supposedly, his or her behavior. By altering physiological and chemical balances, many parents feel that they have observed positive changes in their autistic children, from a calmer demeanor to greater communication abilities. There is an enormous pool of anecdotal evidence among parents about the efficacy of the biomedical approach, indicating the need for more studies.

But currently there are no bona fide scientific, double-blind studies that support many of these popular therapies. In fact, one twelve-week study done by the National Institutes of Health in 2006, as well as a more recent study done by the Mayo Clinic, found there to be little or no change in autistic children who were on the gluten-free, casein-free diet. And unfortunately, certain biomedical interventions have in rare instances caused harm, as in the case of Abubakar Tariq Nadama, a little boy who died in 2005 from an improper chelation procedure (although charges against the doctor were later dropped). In addition to that, many fear a new danger for the world's children should vaccine use decline: the return of deadly childhood diseases such as measles.

It is truly not my purpose to judge anyone. My aim here is to identify this deep divide in the autism community, taking a look at the opposing viewpoints and the impact of this divide on parents and families. In the interest of full disclosure, I myself am not an adherent of the biomedical approaches to autism treatment. I also do not personally believe that vaccines are behind the rise in autism, though perhaps there has been some sort of environmental trigger for some of the cases (numerous medical experts I have spoken with have suggested as much).

Many of the parents who believe that autism can be cured feel that the medical establishment is behind the times at best—and in bed with the pharmaceutical industry at worst. These suspicions spring out of the fear that the pharmaceuticals have pushed an increasing number of vaccines on infants and toddlers, and the doctors who have administered them are covering up the fact that these vaccines have triggered the rise in autism. This community of parents believe that doctors, pharmaceuticals (which are referred to, in Orwellian style, as "Big Pharma"), and government institutions such as the Centers for Disease Control (CDC) each have their own agendas for suppressing the truth about vaccines. They believe that doctors and pharmaceuticals are now desperate to avoid class action suits and that the CDC is trying to avoid admitting culpability (because they've consistently recommended a full schedule of vaccines for infants and toddlers—and thus the spread of the panic).

Kim from Connecticut has three daughters on the spectrum, and feels that one of the reasons for the confusion surrounding treatment approaches, and the resulting mistrust of the medical establishment, is that doctors are closed to nontraditional therapies. "I've taken my girls to every top neurology, genetics, endocrinology, and developmental pediatric specialist from Cleveland to Philadelphia," says Kim. "They often vehemently and condescendingly steer us away from the nontraditional therapies. Why? Because no one has published a double-blind study in a peer-reviewed journal such as JAMA [*Journal of the American Medical Association*]. Virtually none of them have an answer for us," she says.

Kim has become no less than a rabid advocate about exposing the alleged corruption in the medical and pharmaceutical establishments. Her skepticism is born of observing her own daughters' behavior and communication abilities—and many other children's as well—improve under the DAN protocol. "When we pulled all dairy out of her diet, our three-year-old's behavior changed dramatically," Kim told me. "It took time, several months, but she stopped raging, screaming, running around. For our other daughter, the wheat made her completely looped, stoned. She went from writing her name on paper and coloring to lolling about on the floor, eyes glazed during the wheat testing. So out went the gluten." Kim is no longer employed because she must devote so much of her time to taking care of her daughters, whose challenges vary from communication issues to seizures. Even though the testing, costly vitamin supplements, and foods are difficult for the family to afford, she is determined to pursue this treatment because she feels it has helped her daughters.

Heather, like Kim, believes that vaccines caused her son's autism, and feels the same sense of anger and alienation toward the medical community. She witnessed a direct correlation of vaccine with his regression, which her doctors did not validate. "Liam was ahead of the game on language, talking more than his cousin who was a year older than him," says Heather. "He had friends at school, he taught other kids at eighteen months how to do baby signs, he ran around kicking a soccer ball so well that they wanted to bend the rules and have him join a soccer team for kids who were two.

"Then he got his DTP and chicken pox vaccine. He spiked a fever, started screaming at night and not sleeping, developed a huge rash, very irritable, no longer responded to his name all the time, yet he could hear a motorcycle and label the noise as it drove by with the windows closed. He started to have episodes where he would turn white, lips blue and hands purple, and would start to shake. He then started to slowly regress into autism. He became ill *all* the time. If you look at his medical records, it was almost like we were at the doctor's office weekly. Either he was ill, or we were concerned about his not sleeping, his irritability, or the 'episodes' as the doctors called them. Even so, at two years he was still considered advanced in intelligence and speech, but he no longer really engaged in playing with us. I kept thinking maybe it was autism, but I was told by doctors, 'No, he is just delayed, he is too social,' or 'No, he doesn't show this or that symptom.'"

Biomedical approaches aren't helpful for everyone, however, and yet their popularity—and parents' desperation—leads many to try them. Susan, a Rhode Island mom of a fourteen-year-old autistic girl, told me about her experiences with DAN. "We saw a few DAN doctors who would say try such-and-such a vitamin and you'll see results, or try this diet and you will see results. We just didn't see any improvement with those things." Even with no evidence of improvement, parents such as Susan hear of so many autistic children's skills improving through the DAN protocol that they often feel guilty or uncertain about stopping. And no one can give them a definitive recommendation they feel they can trust.

NancyBea did not observe any sort of robust response either when she implemented the DAN protocol for her son. Raising Henry, who is mostly nonverbal and has many challenging behaviors, has been a struggle in which she and her husband, Paul, have been largely on their own. "The biggest problem has been getting adequate help and information," she says. They have spent a good deal of Henry's life wanting desperately to help him, trying many different therapies, from the educational to the biomedical. The DAN protocol was one of those treatments. After a year of expending time, energy, and money, working with a well-recommended doctor to find if her child had food intolerances, physiological imbalances, or allergies, NancyBea called it quits. "The doctor offered test after test. There are literally thousands you can take, every two weeks, for a period of over a year. After the first dozen, we lost interest."

On the other side of the autism divide are those who do not believe that autism can be cured, seeing it as genetically based, a sort of atypical neurological wiring. Those on this side of the divide also want to improve their child's behavior and functioning, but they don't believe that you can eliminate the symptoms of autism, just perhaps reduce them. They see autism as a condition you live with and accommodate.

Many on the autism-acceptance side of the divide view the spectrum as adding color and variety to life, part of the natural diversity of life that also gave us brains like Einstein's. They believe that autism is a way of being, the symptoms of which should be ameliorated if possible, but only for the comfort of the person with autism, to allow him to express himself better, to increase his quality of life and ability to be happy. They feel that society must also change, and must become more tolerant of autistic behaviors and the challenges that arise from being neurologically atypical. They see autistic people as a minority group deserving accommodation and respect. This movement is often called "neurodiversity," and it takes the position that our society should stop seeing autistic people (and other neurologically atypical folks) as flawed, broken, or inferior to others.

Though I am more in the neurodiversity or autism-acceptance camp, I empathize with both viewpoints, knowing and admiring people in both camps. And the truth is, at some level, most parents are in both camps at once. We all want to help our children to be able to do more and live better, and we also love and cherish our kids just the way they are.

Yet many parents feel that one group is a threat to the other. Those in the neurodiversity camp seem to think that if you want to cure autism, then you must not be able to accept and value the person with autism. They feel insulted by the "curebies," who, in the never-ending search for a cure, subject autistic people to all sorts of demanding treatments, some of which are not supported by science. They make allegations of "quackery" on a regular basis, which can't possibly encourage any kind of productive dialogue. They also ask, justifiably, "What is the impact of continually conveying the message to your child that he is fundamentally diseased and must be changed? And what will be the impact on society of so many people refusing vaccines?"

In turn, some of those who believe that biomedical interventions can bring about a cure feel that autism stole their children from them. They see the neurodiversity community as irresponsible and negligent. These parents ask, "How can you not try to help your child in any way you can? Why would you *want* him to be disabled?" There is an equal degree of harsh name-calling and bloody blogging from this side, too.

NancyBea explains how it has been for her, as a curebie-cum-autism-accepter: "People want to assume there is a cure, that if you work hard enough, you will be able to 'fix' whatever is wrong. And so, by implication, if you haven't, you are either lazy or stupid or have some sick wish to keep your child under-functioning." Raquel suggests that at the heart of this anguished divide is the fact that some children diagnosed with autism do improve greatly in communication, sensory, and behavioral skills, and so many parents tie that to the therapies they've employed. Even though dramatic improvement doesn't occur with most children, there is always the hope that it will for yours, but only—as Raquel points out—*if you are doing it right.*

Both groups in the autism community make important points, but I and so many others are very frustrated with the two groups' frequent inability to see any good in the other. Indeed, there is at times a virulent hatred between the groups; some people I know on either side are frequently reviled on blogs. Some have even had threats made against them.

I understand so well, on one hand, why a parent would want to reduce or eliminate their child's autism, and it is *not* because they cannot see how wonderful the child is, autism and all. They most likely believe that their child is being prevented from living up to his or her fullest potential, and they want to change that. Also, some of the behaviors that can come with autism, such as running off, inexplicable tantrums, and unpredictable aggression, can wreak havoc in a family and be very dangerous for the child himself.

In turn, it's appropriate and helpful for the neurodiversity crowd to point out the potential hazards and negative message of subjecting our children to treatment after treatment. Those parents who do not seek a cure cannot be painted as monsters who don't care about their children. Not all interventions are beneficial. Both sides have valid viewpoints. Both sides love their children. But the end result of the autism divide is that many autism parents feel judged and criticized, not only by the world at large but by other members of the autism community, which only adds to the difficulties we face when trying to help our children and enjoy our lives.

Mastering the Learning Curve and Decision-Making Process of Choosing Autism Therapies

- Ask your evaluating physician for recommendations of books and approaches. Do not let your doctor off the hook if he or she gives you the kind of vague advice that I received ("You'll know when it's working").

- Be selective in your online research. Look for Web sites that end in ".gov" or ".edu." The government sites, such as those of the Centers for Disease Control (cdc.gov) and National Institutes of Health (nih.gov), are reliable and have many links to support services and federal programs. University research tends to be trustworthy as well. The University of North Carolina has an autism information center worth checking out: the Treatment and Education of Autistic and Related Communication-Handicapped Children, at teacch.com.

- The Autism Society of America (autism-society.org) is neither a government-based nor a university-based organization, but it is a venerable institution that has grown with the times. The ASA has autistic people on their board, and they run a very comprehensive conference every year and in a different city each time.

- If you find an alternative treatment:

1. Ask if the treatment involves anything physiological that may conflict in any way with the medications your child may be currently taking.

2. Talk to a few parents whom you trust to get a sense from them of whether the approach is worthwhile. Have they tried it? For how long? With what results?

3. If you are still interested in the therapy, try to find out what is involved for the family and you in terms of location and investments of money and time. See if your insurance can cover this. In some states there is Medicare coverage for therapies, especially for young children. In fact, as of the printing of this book, the proposed federal health care reform bill may call for insurance companies to provide coverage of certain autism therapies, such as ABA, Applied Behavioral Analysis, one of the most commonly used treatments. Look up "Medicaid" or "Medicare autism waivers" on wikipedia.org to see what your state offers.

4. If all of these steps check out, ask yourself if this is something that you agree with philosophically. Do you believe the approach will help your child have an easier life? Is it something that will most likely make him happier, more skilled, or give him other benefits?

- Take a look at books on both sides of the autism divide. For example, Dr. Paul A. Offit's book *Autism's False Prophets* debunks some popular theories and treatments. (Keep in mind, however, that this book is hated by those on the "cure" side.) David Kirby's *Evidence of Harm* lays out the entire vaccine-injury theory (and is hated by folks on the "neurodiversity" side).

GETTING PERSPECTIVE

Why would parents put themselves through all the therapy-chasing, particularly of the unproven sort, for an uncertain result? The answer has to do with the nature of the grief process, the lack of direction in the field, and the perplexing, very individualized nature of autism. "Searching for a cure is part of the process of coming to terms with the diagnosis, any diagnosis, and what it means both for the child and for the family," says Cindy N. Ariel, PhD, psychologist, clinical director at Alternative Choices in Philadelphia, and coauthor of *Voices from the Spectrum*. "Doing everything possible for their child helps parents to feel somewhat better about themselves by taking an active part in helping their child and maintaining hope for the future of the child and of the family."

Because autism affects so many aspects of a person—cognitive function, sensory processing, social ability, language capacity—in such different ways, parents are highly motivated to do something, anything, and quickly, to help. The unresolved state of treatment makes parents unwilling pioneers, forced to journey into uncharted territory. And, arduous though it may be, approaches such as DAN provide a detailed map to follow. Parents want to feel like they are doing everything possible, when in fact, these things may not help their particular child. I know that I still feel certain pangs, and sometimes great remorse, when I think about the strategies I have not tried for Nat simply because they were too hard for me to manage. I am still prone to wondering, even obsessively at times, if there is more I could or should be doing to make Nat become higher functioning.

Dr. Eileen Costello, pediatrician and coauthor of the book *Quirky Kids,* says that with a disorder as difficult and comprehensive as autism, "You don't want to leave any stone unturned. Parents with kids with a developmental disorder are more desperate. They think there must be things they can do to undo it." To Costello, trying many alternative approaches, no matter how difficult, expensive, or unproven, provides autism parents with a certain sense of control and even satisfaction that they are doing everything they can. If a child improves when on the gluten-free, casein-free diet, or on any other approach, parents then believe that it was their chosen approach that was responsible, and not the myriad of other factors, such as developmental growth, environmental changes, or even a more optimistic parent.

But who is to say they are wrong? Autism parents strive to master scientific theories of how the brain works, pushing past the qualified, seemingly wishy-washy recommendations of their doctors. They enter the arena of anecdotal evidence and the uncomfortable nether regions of pseudoscience and uncertainty, where Internet support groups supplant physicians' recommendations. They feel forced to keep trying, emptying bank accounts, straining an already suffering family, and setting themselves up for possible failure.

If specialists can't agree on the right methods to begin with, the parent is all the more subject to taking drastic action. Dr. Tim Buie, of Massachusetts General Hospital, says, "Someone is going to have to do a better job. Traditional medicine needs to put some science behind it. The traditional doc sees the kid and makes the diagnosis, saying, 'Here's the ABA provider. Good luck.' [Applied Behavior Analysis is one of the most commonly recommended treatments.] You're taught a kid hits himself in the head because he's trying to turn up his level of attention. It gets written off as a behavior when actually the cause might be physical, such as an intestinal disorder, a headache, or any number of other things. That's just a mistake."

Dr. Buie believes the lack of conclusive research is at the heart of the autism parents' relentless, sometimes reckless, approach to helping their children. Buie, in combination with Harvard University and Massachusetts General Hospital, has been conducting a study called the Autism Project, in which scientists are striving to uncover the biomedical bases of autism by looking at autistic children with suspected gastrointestinal problems, treating the GI issues, and studying which, if any, autistic symptoms were alleviated. The Project has evaluated some one thousand autistic children for the study, and some of the findings may give weight to the thinking of the DAN doctors and parents.

Nevertheless, Buie feels that there is not yet enough reasonable science being applied toward children with autism, from any quarter. Because of this untenable, confusing situation, Buie envisions a much broader responsibility on the part of practitioners and researchers. "Treatment centers should vet out consistent responses. When you treat large numbers of kids, put together a database." The responsibility of practitioners should be to go beyond the quick answer, the quick fix, and figure out why a given treatment worked for a given portion of the autistic population. Says Buie, "If we say that the last study that looked at Secretin [an enzyme once believed to cure autism] helped 20 percent of the kids and therefore doesn't work, we're making a mistake. We shouldn't have expectations a single treatment is going to help across the board." As it is, parents are left to figure things out for themselves. The meaning of the diversity of characteristics in the autism spectrum is perhaps the missing piece of the treatment puzzle, as Buie indicates.

What all this boils down to is that autism parents frequently feel a great amount of guilt. The guilt of not doing enough can be *the* motivator for many autism parents. NancyBea says, "To me, one of the horrors of trying to sift through all the hundreds of possible 'cures' on offer is wondering if I should keep going, if the next thing I try might do the job. And the practitioners will tell you 'it may not work, but it may.'"

Underlying all of these stories and observations are some very real feelings of inadequacy and despair. Parents' feelings of helplessness and confusion should be looked at carefully and individually and treated as a genuine, ongoing problem, and not simply as collateral damage. Too frequently, parents of an autistic child present with symptoms of depression, and therapists and physicians may write it off as a temporary by-product of initially dealing with the child's diagnosis.

Perhaps finding a balance between chasing therapies, on the one hand, and accepting and simply enjoying one's child, and one's life, on the other, eventually allows parents to slow down the frenzied search and alleviate some of these depressive symptoms. Dr. Ariel believes that "by the later years, families have developed coping skills and the families reach a balance that includes naturally living with a child with a disability"—in other words, accepting the child's issues as being a part of the family life.

Dr. Costello has found the same thing in her experience: "Most families feel that by the time the kids have become teenagers, things are much better than they were in the early years." Those who feel OK about their family issues, however, likely feel that way *because of their own attitude of acceptance* rather than because of any outward improvement or changes in the child. Dr. O'Brien's research bears some of this out. In her findings, the group of moms who tended *not* to get depressed had "a tendency to focus on how the child is doing day-to-day; they get pleasure out of what's happening now instead of what the child might have been . . . they take joy in many aspects of their relationships, but they are experiencing all these feelings all at once, dealing with both the positive and the negative all the time." In other words, the more an autism mother or father is able to accept and embrace the reality of their challenging life and child, the more likely they are to be happy.

Karen from Ohio is one such autism parent who moved from a terrible crisis point to acceptance and great happiness, all in a few short months. Conor, her son, is only around three years old, but Karen has learned a lifetime's worth of wisdom in those few years. She wrote to me about the excruciating early days, when she had a newborn, a newly diagnosed autistic two-year-old son, and a four-year-old. "I was completely devastated by the diagnosis. It was the shattered-dreams phenomenon. I got over that part fairly quickly, and began getting to the very confusing work of finding services for Conor. There were so many options, and varying opinions, that this was an extremely difficult part of the process. Meanwhile, our third child was born. The idea of having a newborn and a child with autism was more than I could bear. The only concept I had of autism at that point was what you see in movies, television shows, and so on. It was those horribly painted pictures that kept me from moving toward acceptance."

Karen's early days, though fifteen years apart from mine, were nearly exactly the same as mine and so many others I know. "Eventually, we got all of his services lined up," she continued. "There was speech therapy and occupational therapy on Mondays, and Early Intervention on Tuesdays. There was also some physical therapy in there for a while. Meanwhile, I was being bombarded by the various 'cures' and treatments. The first six to twelve months were very overwhelming. Add to that a newborn who was an extremely fussy baby."

Despite lining up all the necessary therapies and inter-ventions, Karen was still suffering. "Conor seemed very unhappy," she said. "He would crawl into the stroller basket and stay there for hours at a time. My husband was spending an excessive amount of time on the computer doing research." Karen's husband believed fervently, much more so than Karen, that there was not a cure for autism. "I was left to sort out my feelings on my own. It was a terrible struggle. I could tell all of the therapy and work was making Conor unhappy, but I was terrified to take it away from him and jeopardize his progress. At that point, I was still looking for the *right* combination of treatments. I was also extremely reluctant to talk to my husband about what I was feeling, for fear of him going on an anti-cure tirade. I was trying to sort out my feelings without being tainted by his." Karen's experience of the great divide between those autism parents who seek out a cure and those who see autism as permanent and neurological was horribly personal because she and her husband were at odds at that time.

"Then came my own personal rock bottom," Karen wrote. "I actually felt that I was rejecting Conor. Not because of his diagnosis, but because he paid no attention to what I could offer him. He wouldn't look at me. He never noticed when I came home from work. He would say 'Dadadadada,' but not even a hint of 'Mama.' It felt like I may as well not even exist. I found myself just ignoring him, and giving all my attention to my other two children, the ones who were happy to accept my love and affection. This is where the terrible guilt began. I was so disconnected from Conor, and had less and less desire to make the effort. I sought help from my primary care doctor, and was started on an antidepressant. This seemed to help some, but I still felt the terrible guilt. I was barely hanging on. Eventually all the emotional turmoil affected my physical health. I came down with bilateral pneumonia, for which part of my treatment included painkillers. Those painkillers gave me a sense of euphoria that I hadn't felt in quite a while. But they also contributed to my downward spiral. There was one point where I was sitting on the bedroom floor, sobbing, unable to stop. I told my husband that I just didn't see what the whole point to life is; what is the point of me being here when I can't even connect with my own child?"

But at this, the worst point in their lives so far, Karen and her husband, Jack, must have realized what they had to do—and they found the strength to do it. They began opening up to each other. They would have long conversations about their opposing views on autism, and everything else. They also got some counseling. "Through these long talks," Karen said, "I learned to communicate my thoughts and feelings without fear of ridicule or contempt. I also came to the realization that Conor is my son, and that I was perfectly happy with exactly who he is. I realized that there was not a single thing I would change about him. It's not that I love him in spite of his differences, but that I love him *because* of his differences."

This catharsis of Karen's sounded similar to a realization I had when Nat was twelve years old. Back then I was annoyed by his loud, fake laughter. But one day I suddenly understood, without a doubt, that this was Nat's attempt to get my attention and to connect with me. And nothing was ever the same after that. I began seeing Nat as a person—a person with eccentricities and annoying quirks, but a whole, human being nonetheless. It still hurts to admit how I must have been seeing him before that point. But at least I no longer feel that way!

This was, of course, an extreme epiphany for Karen as well, being able to see Conor for who he really was, and also to feel suddenly so happy with that. Almost immediately, a new equanimity followed for Karen, a kind of calm and a sense of what was important for their family's happiness. "I stopped being concerned with how much therapy he was receiving. If anything, I wanted to stop *all* of his therapy. It was extremely intrusive, and it didn't seem to be helping him. The most amazing part was that when I achieved this complete acceptance, that is when Conor really started to flourish developmentally. Within weeks he was saying new words, running to the door calling 'Mommeeeeee' when I came home from work, being more interactive with the other family members. He just seemed happy again. It was at that point that I knew that my acceptance of him was the most important therapy he could ever receive."

Karen has learned a great deal about her own values and wisdom from all this. "I now feel sorry for the parents who are spending all their time and money on treatment after treatment. I feel bad for the kids who are being dragged all over town, just to try another treatment (quack or not), because their parents haven't figured out how to just stop, take a breath, and enjoy the small moments. Eighteen months ago I couldn't even think the word *autism* without welling up. Now, I shout it from the rooftops. I probably offend many people by telling them they may be on the spectrum, but I always follow it up with a 'Hey, by the way, that was a compliment.'

Both NancyBea and Karen may have recently reached the blessed point of peace and acceptance. Karen's children are so young, and yet she felt completely turned around and empowered by her experience of hitting rock bottom with Conor. For some parents, getting to this kind of healthy state has nothing to do with the child's age or intensity of diagnosis. Progress toward peace of mind may have more to do with a parent's ability to let go of the need to change his or her child.

NancyBea has been at it so long, she now understands her son's strengths and weaknesses. In the past year or so she has stopped the crazed running after therapies. She is now focused instead on fine-tuning Henry's medication and his education program, a combination of approaches that incorporate some principles of Applied Behavior Analysis along with the use of visuals and a highly organized schedule and physical environment to help Henry focus on his learning. Whether it's the approach, her level of acceptance, or her new, more relaxed state of mind, things are better than they used to be for the family. "These days when he comes home, he's in a good mood," she says with a satisfied sigh. That, so far, is the best evidence for autism parents that something is "working," and that perhaps they are doing enough.

3

Spending Time with Our Kids
—and Enjoying It

I'M NOT PROUD TO ADMIT THIS, but for the longest time I felt that the only way I could really have fun was just with my husband or with my own friends, not with my children. I was not a sit-on-the-floor-and-play-with-cars kind of mom, particularly because my firstborn only liked to line them up and look at them, with his thumb in his mouth. But even when Max and Ben came along, "pway wif me" were words that made me feel dull and sleepy. I don't know why; I had a lot on my plate, I guess. Maybe I thought their expectations were higher than they actually were. It wasn't until I was an older mom that I grew into my role as Fun Muse, or at least Willing Companion.

Over the years, I figured out that fun with my kids did not have to mean dissolving into their world of bad guys, monsters, Transformers, spaceships, and so on. Fun can be bigger than that—or smaller. Fun could simply be lying around on a couch, half reading and half having a thumb wrestle, with any of my three boys, Nat included. Or we could simply take a walk and look for animals. Five minutes, five hours, whatever we felt like would do. One of the best things I ever realized as a mother was that I could also simply say, "OK, darling, I'm done for now," and to know that it was OK. Discovering that was a huge relief, an important step toward taking care of myself. In addition to what it did for me, asserting my needs was an important message and model for my boys. It gave my children the experience of not getting what they wanted all the time, of figuring out what else they could do, and last but not least, of seeing me as a separate person with needs of my own. One preschool teacher I met summed it up like this: "You need to let children develop their 'struggle muscle.'"

Sometimes, though, I learned that stretching myself a little, and trying something my kid wanted to do even if I didn't, could end up being fun. I actually found I was very good at building with Legos, for instance (as long as I got to use the cool, translucent, neon-colored ones) because Max wanted me to design different lands with him. Designing unusual worlds fit my interests more than building the typical prepackaged Lego fare of spaceships or shark-shaped submarines. This discovery crystallized for me particularly as Nat grew older, when it was easier to predict what he would like to do, and what might then be a successful outing. The downside, however, was that although things were easier to anticipate, they were not always easy to get going.

In his late teenage years, Nat was usually happy to lie around on the couch all day. One summer afternoon, however, I became fed up with seeing him lying there. But I also did not feel up to doing anything about it, because I wanted to go for a run. I could have simply gone for my run, leaving him there, because it was a Sunday, and Ned was home. But that seemed wrong. So I asked Nat if he wanted to run with me. To my surprise, he leaped to his feet immediately.

I took him to the town reservoir, which has a gravel track around its perimeter. I wondered what he would make of it all—the ducks, the geese, the people. Or they of him. Nat loves to proclaim his joy to the world by waving his arms and talking loudly to himself. When we got there, and before I could finish stretching, he had taken off, in a gigantic loping stride, right through the middle of the geese. I started running, but at a much slower pace (I couldn't help it, I'm just not that fast).

Nat got way ahead of me, which was OK until I saw that he was approaching the pump house, a small shed near the bank of the reservoir where the path becomes much narrower. There were two people passing through this narrow pathway at the same time as Nat. I tried to catch up, gulping air and pumping my legs hard against the gravel, but I could not get to him in time.

There was no problem, however; he passed through swiftly and smoothly.

Nat kept going, but ran out of steam by the second mile; he's more of a sprinter than a distance runner. Now I was ahead of him. I dodged the geese and lengthened my stride. I felt my body settle into the exertion, and my breathing started to even out. Feeling the sun on my shoulders, I turned around every so often to check on Nat, but he was happy enough to stay about ten paces behind me, talking and arm waving. I suddenly felt so proud of him.

Eventually I slowed down to a walk so he could catch up to me. "OK, darling?" I asked.

"OK," he answered. His hand bumped mine. I didn't respond, assuming it was an accident from his ever-moving arms. But then he did it again.

Then I realized that he wanted to hold my hand. That was a first. I grasped his fingers and held firm. We walked together hand in hand, finishing our lap. I don't know if you would describe this outing as "fun," but it certainly made me happy.

No matter the age of your kids, there are ways to have fun—ways that both parents and kids can enjoy. Maybe this is obvious, but it's important to be reminded of it and keep it in mind during trying times. Too often we let ourselves get dragged under by caregiving obligations, and we forget about simple happiness. Your fun may mean choosing an ordinary, no-fail activity, such as a trip to the playground, where you might bring along a crossword puzzle for yourself—unless, that is, playgrounds are particularly difficult places for your autistic child. (For instance, my friend Sheila's son used to take every opportunity to scale the high fences that surrounded our park.) Having a few moments to yourself might give you the energy to then enjoy the next moment, when your child needs your attention again.

Ed from Ohio says, "Sometimes we take our son to the park and he uses all the equipment. Sometimes, he will just walk around the tennis courts thirty times. It's not all fun— but it's not all bad, either." This may not sound like much of a rave, but the thing is, parenting any kid is like that: not all fun, and not all bad.

Donna is a mom from Massachusetts who has learned to enjoy her son by seeing things from his point of view: "He loves to jump on a trampoline, ride his bike, and slide down those large, inflatable slides on the moonwalks that every kid seems to have at his or her birthday party." This past summer her family took a trip overseas. Before the plane took off, the flight attendant explained about emergency landings. Christopher appeared very interested and seemed to be following along in his own safety pamphlet. "He suddenly tugged on my arm to get my attention to show me the illustration of the emergency landing, and the people sliding down the inflated emergency chute," says Donna. "At that point, he asked, in a perfectly worded sentence (which made me feel very proud of his expressive-language skills), if he could 'have a turn down the big slide.' My husband and I chuckled at this sincere request, but we also made sure to keep him away from the exit doors!" Donna and her husband were tickled by Christopher's way of seeing things, so different from theirs, and thus the plane ride was a bonding experience rather than a stressful one.

No matter how difficult it can be sometimes with children, especially those on the spectrum, many autism parents summon up the energy from somewhere to get their kids out into the world.

"Our kids deserve a childhood!" Kim, my friend in Connecticut wrote to me. When I asked her what she does for fun with them, she had a lot to say: "The kids love swimming and the house we just rented has a pool. That was an easy treat—going to the town pool was too difficult with all three, as you can imagine." Kim also says that her kids love amusement parks and carousels. "Shocking, isn't it," she says jokingly, "they love to spin!" She summed up her thoughts like this: "We try to do everything any parent does with their kids. We might go for a shorter period of time or less frequently, but we've never let autism trap us in our home."

Some parents find serenity and fun with family members who truly understand, like NancyBea. "Every two years we have an extended family reunion in Wisconsin. Henry just loves it, and my family will watch him for a bit." There are swimming pools at the family reunion, which Henry loves like nothing else. "He just reeks of chlorine by the end of the week! My dream is to be able to go to a family camp that provides supports for kids with special needs. You'd know they're having a great time at the pool while you're off on a hike." NancyBea has not found such a camp yet, but feels she has glimpses of it in her extended family get-togethers.

Some parents are able to be more adventurous, due to their children's cooperativeness and other factors such as financial resources, a strong marriage, and extra help. Cathy from Connecticut has four kids, one of whom is seven years old and has PDD-NOS (which, in her optimistic way, she calls "autism lite"). Talking more seriously, she says, "I had no idea that parenthood could be so painful." But she is determined to have a good quality of life despite that pain and struggle. She and her husband have tried to make a good life for their entire family, which is complicated, given that one of the four children is a toddler.

With four kids to balance, Cathy has had a big challenge. It is important to her to focus enough of her attention on all four of her children, so she has an au pair for help. But mostly she credits her children for the family's success—including Jack, her autistic son. "He doesn't have a lot of temper tantrums," Cathy says, which she knows is a huge plus for the family. Having successfully survived Nat's years and years of unpredictability, outbursts, and tantrums, I can happily say I feel the same way, that the way Nat is now—mostly calm and willing to try new things—is truly a gift. However, at times I still have that tightness in my throat, that old familiar fear that his flexibility and peacefulness could disappear at a moment's notice. But although this kind of tension hovers over most autism families, there is also an element of intense pleasure when it all works out, a feeling of "High five! We did it! Yes!" that normal families might not experience.

Cathy, like me, sees her satisfying family moments as a group achievement. "All of our family members play a role in the family's happiness; all can do something to improve things, one way or another." Cathy keeps in mind that the dynamics among her children are key to their happiness. "The kids are a gift to one another."

Cathy's family has even managed to go to Hawaii on a vacation. She explained to me how the various arrangements she made for her trip helped the vacation be successful and fun: "The trip (like everything) required planning akin to a military maneuver! I was careful to choose two flights that were at a good time of day and were equal in length." Using DVD players, snacks, and the requisite potty breaks filled the time on board the plane. Another nice thing for Cathy's family was their ability to bring along an au pair.

For Cathy, and other autism moms she and I know, the au pair solution is a godsend. During the application and interview process, au pairs can indicate whether they would be interested in working with a special-needs child. Cathy has had her au pairs sit in on an ABA session or two, and then they get a good feel for what to do, at least enough to give a mother a break now and then.

Of course, not everyone can afford an au pair, which costs approximately $15,000 a year. But perhaps there are ways to create a similar setup. If you live near a college or university, for example, you might be able to have a college student board with you, in exchange for child care (once you have thoroughly checked out his or her credentials). A high school kid, too, can often work out, but as a mother's helper rather than for respite from your autistic child. We have also employed some teenage girls to hang out with Ben, our youngest, while I focused on Nat, playing with him or taking him to the park or to a movie. High schoolers often tend to charge much less. Any of your helpers might turn out to be people you could consider bringing with you on a vacation, possibly without pay if the vacation itself is enough of an incentive; it's worth asking about.

If your family can't make it to a big vacation such as Hawaii, Disney World and Disneyland seem to be the vacation of choice for many autism parents. Kim told me that her family's best vacation in years was to Disney; Grandma was able to come along. With a lot of planning, it worked out beautifully. "Since we're on the GFCF diet, food is always an issue. I packed a ton of food and consulted with the chef at the Marriott in Orlando. They were able to prepare foods for the girls. Because of the prevalence of celiac disease and food allergies, most hotels can handle special diets."

Maribel is another mom who also found that Disney was very accommodating for her family's needs: "We do not get to go often—finances make that very hard. It took us six years to get to Florida to see family and to see Mickey. Last year we went back. It was our second vacation, and it was so much fun. Disney is an absolute dream: the dietary options and the Fast Pass make it easier for us. [The Fast Pass is a system that allows you, with your admission ticket, to register for a ride that has a long wait. All you do is show up at the designated time.] Granted, the first time we went we took it in small doses because Gabe couldn't withstand the sensory overload, but this last time he was able to deal with it so much better."

Like Maribel's, my family did better the second time we attempted Disney, because the boys were older and more adept at travel and at taking care of themselves. I'm glad we didn't give up after the first trip there, when Max was two and Nat was four. Max was so young at the time that he even fell asleep on my shoulder in the Haunted Mansion ride! This gave us a good laugh; but Nat seemed so out of it a lot of the time, too, which did not make us happy. The weather didn't cooperate either. One particular image that stands out in my mind is of a very cold and raw boat ride over to Pleasure Island. I remember feeling so tired of the effort I was making to have fun. Two years later, at four and six, however, having been there once, Nat and Max were able to enjoy it much more. Familiarity with something helps any child adjust the next time around, especially if it is a fairly universal favorite, such as Disney World.

Even if your autistic child is very young or very challenging, there are still ways to travel and have fun together. Maribel also enjoys simple activities with Gabriel. "Because Gabe has so many sensory and gross motor issues to deal with, we make sure he gets a lot of play time. We do obstacle races, play in the pool, use the swings, go for walks, ride scooters and bikes. In the summer we go to the beach or to a local pond to feed the ducks. Board games (simpler ones, nothing overwhelming) are good too, and lately we have been playing charades." Like my run at the reservoir, doing everyday leisure activities can take on satisfying, joyful meaning when they become things you can enjoy dependably with your autistic child.

Jennie is a young mom from Florida who has three children, two of whom are on the spectrum. Like Maribel and Ed, Jennie feels that going simple is best for a family like hers. Her list of favorite family activities includes going to the playground, the beach, and birthday parties; picking fruit at a farm; feeding animals; "basically just anything out of the house where they can interact with society."

Heather is the mother of Liam, nearly five. She describes her typical state of mind this way: "It's like being a rubber band stretched to capacity and having someone come over and pluck at it." Even so, she has found that long trips work for them because they exposed Liam to vacations early in life: "Liam loves the airport, loves to fly, and loves the adventure of new places, so for us vacations really aren't that bad. We bring 'fly presents' on board the plane for him to open if he is bored. These are small, inexpensive, wrapped toys that provide him with some kind of activity. We also bring a portable DVD player, which keeps him very happy. We use that on the plane and in the car for long trips."

Sometimes food is the most challenging aspect of having fun together. Like many autism families, Heather's kids are on the GFCF diet. She thinks that the right snack, foods, and a way to prepare them on the go help the family have a good time. We, too, focus on food when we go on vacations with Nat, Max, and Ben, even though they aren't on a special diet but instead are just picky eaters. On the second of our Disney vacations, for example, Max and Nat would only eat French fries and dry cereal. Heather described for me how she manages the food: "We pack a huge cooler and make sure we have a kitchenette and a fridge where we are staying. We map out where we can find a Whole Foods or other natural foods store close to where we are staying, and call them ahead of time to see what they carry. We ask them to hold some things for us as well, and they are usually pretty accommodating. I send some frozen food overnight to our destination as well."

As for fun closer to home, though her life is admittedly chaotic, Heather tries a wide range of activities with Liam. "We sing and dance, play tag, go for walks in the woods, swim, play soccer, play superheroes, cook together, play hide-and-seek, go kayaking, and go to the aquarium."

When we need to be at home, during Nat's difficult phases, we still have to find a way to have fun, no matter what we're struggling with. But how do you have fun with the family when you can't leave the house or go anywhere special? Amy, a Washington mom who is in the military, likes to play competitive video games with her kids, taking the "if you can't beat 'em, join 'em" approach. "We got a Wii," she told me. "I love playing it with my oldest son. It's good ole family fun! I like to get that competitive streak going every now and then!"

For me, baking is an easy, fun activity with built-in positive reinforcement and plenty of steps for everyone. And, of course, following steps is a favorite of Nat's.

Here's one of our favorite backing activities, making a Spooky Cake Hand. (Warning: This unusual recipe is not on *anyone's* diet!)

Spooky Cake Hand

INGREDIENTS

10 ReeseSticks wafer bars
1/2 can vanilla frosting
Green food coloring (enough to achieve
    a sickly-green skin tone)
10 Milk Duds
5 or 6 red gummies
2 Hostess Twinkies

When we made this, Max cut up the peanut butter sticks into appropriate finger sizes. I cut a Twinkie in half to form the hand and cut the ends off another for the severed wrist. Nat colored the frosting green, and then we frosted the whole mess. I drew knuckles with a sharp knife, cleaning the point after every mark. Max then placed Milk Duds for the finger-nails, and then I ripped up some red gummies for the blood drops!

For other (healthier) recipe ideas to try with or for your kids, consult *Mom's Big Book of Baking* by Lauren Chattman, or *Disney's Family Cookbook* by Deanna F. Cook. The latter has many projects similar to the Spooky Cake Hand.

If you are following special diets, autism mom and blogger Kristina Chew recommends the Vegan Chef Web site (veganchef.com), which even has a recipe for gluten-free gingerbread! And Kim from Connecticut suggests *The Encyclopedia of Dietary Interventions for the Treatment of Autism and Related Disorders* by Karyn Seroussi and Lisa Lewis, PhD. *Nourishing Hope for Autism* by Julie Matthews (nourishing hope.com) is another good diet info book.

So happiness with the kids can be small, close at hand, simple, and straightforward. Sometimes all that's required is a little risk taking and letting go; sometimes it is only about noticing and being satisfied with a small triumph. Alice from Texas has three-and-a-half-year-old twins with a diagnosis of autism and mental retardation. She told me how she is able to stay sane and happy: She celebrates any of the boys' achievements, no matter how small. "When we got the mental retardation diagnosis, it didn't seem like we were going forward. Then they started the ABA. They learned their letters, they learned their numbers. That is huge for us!" Her bouncy voice confirmed her happiness. "I keep getting pleasantly surprised," she said. "They're little, they're not a problem. They're real happy kids." Her children's happiness equals her own; the one state leads to the other.

Sometimes designating one particular time to be family fun time (Saturday afternoon, for example) can help children to adjust to new activities and to have fun outside of the house, because it introduces an element of predictability. Julie, a violinist and writer from Massachusetts, has three children, the oldest two of whom are on the spectrum. "We're really only starting to have fun as a family on a consistent basis," she says. "Recently we've instituted family fun day on Saturdays—we always try to do something fun as a family.

We've gone apple picking, tried a few different crafts, and baked and decorated cookies so far."

Julie says she's figured out a few almost no-fail strategies for fun with the kids. "We go to my in-laws' cottage several times each summer. It's a familiar environment, a home away from home, really. We bring favorite toys and foods, and write out schedules when the kids need them." She went on to say that things have been improving for them, now that the kids are older (Abby is 7, Brian is 4, and Timmy is 3) and they are now finished with diapers and off baby food. Any parent knows what a difference that makes!

During Nat's positive, easier phases I feel energetic and optimistic; these are often the best times to expand the family repertoire and try something new—in a carefully planned way, of course. An important component of planning with Nat involves creating what I call "Nat Books" or "Crisis Stories." I created this parenting strategy seventeen years ago to aid us in a difficult trip to my aunt's for Thanksgiving. I have since learned that many educators recommend a similar strategy, called "social stories." The Nat Books are illustrated and personalized for him, where he's the main character going through a particular new experience. These stories help Nat learn how to get through upcoming events that are new or difficult, for example, starting a new school, moving to a new house, making it through a large social gathering, and so on. In these stories I help him to understand what's going to happen, what behavior will be appropriate, what he might say to others, and even how he might feel and what he can do about it. You can make social stories about every aspect of an outing or an event. Whether it is the first day of school or going on a vacation, describe it all: the school bus, the classroom schedule, the teacher's name. Or if it is a vacation, the long lines at security at the airport, the food choices.

How to Write a Crisis Story

1. Assemble your materials: heavy paper for the front and back covers, pen, tape.

2. Write a draft of what you are trying to convey to your child. Think of the words he typically uses, or the words he understands. Be as precise and simple as you can. Here is an example:

   Tomorrow Jane is going to Grandma's birthday party! Jane will drive in the car for a long time to get to Grandma's house.

   When Jane gets to Grandma's house, she will give Grandma a hug.

   Jane will sit at Grandma's table with Mom and Dad and they will eat lunch. Jane will stay calm and quiet at the table. After lunch, Jane will look at her books for a little while.

   Grandma will say, "Come in and sing 'Happy Birthday'!" Jane will sing "Happy Birthday" to Grandma.

After the song, Jane will eat one piece of birthday cake.

After Jane eats, she will look at her books some more.

Jane does not like waiting, and she might feel a little mad. Jane can stay calm, and ask for a story, a walk, or a jump [or similarly appropriate bit of sensory relief, if sitting still is a problem], and also remember that they will go home soon and that everything is all right.

Jane, Mom, and Dad will get in the car and go home.

---

3. Once you have your text, find photos of the family to illustrate the story. You can also cut up or photoshop images to make it appear as if one person is standing with another if you need to.

4. Write out your final draft on heavy paper, breaking up the story page by page to keep it simple, and tape on the illustrations. You can bind your book together with staples or by using a report cover (available in most drugstores and stationery stores)—or in whatever way you can think of.

5. Read the book to your child as many times as she will allow, so that she is very comfortable with the text and thus the concept of the event.

6. You can learn more about social stories from teacher and author Carol Gray, thegraycenter.org, or check out examples of the books I've made at susansenator.com/crisisstory.html.

The success of our first "crisis story" led to the creation of many more such stories. They have become more sophisticated as Nat has matured, and often we don't use pictures. But for very unusual, momentous events, we still use photos to give him the visual aid.

During a recent summer, a crisis story helped Nat prepare for sleepaway camp, an extreme-sports camp in Aspen specifically designed for the needs of autistic children. But before we even got close to thinking about the crisis story, we had to do lot of research on the camp and planning, being very organized and thorough if this was going to work out for Nat. It was such a new and unusual undertaking (sleeping away from home, taking an airplane, living with strangers for the week, being in a very different location from home).

To get this adventure going, the first thing I did was to talk to the director a few times by phone, to determine with her if the camp was a good fit for Nat's needs. I asked questions about staff-to-camper ratios, profiles and ages of campers, discipline policies, sleeping quarters, how they administer medications. I liked the director's openness and willingness to accommodate Nat. I loved the philosophy of the camp, which was to cater specifically to kids on the autistic spectrum—all types of ASD.

The plan was that while Nat was there, I would go with Ned and the boys on a trip around Colorado: our first vacation without Nat, without autism. We needed that. I needed that. So we were all greatly looking forward to this, even though I think secretly none of us actually believed it would happen. Still, I sent in the deposit and began making reservations.

By the time June rolled around, I was questioning my decision, and my sanity. Sometimes Ned would also say that maybe we should cancel everything, which is unusual for him; once he commits to a plan of action, he nearly always follows through. So I knew that this meant we were really stretching ourselves.

I wondered how all five of us would fly four hours to Denver and then drive several more hours through the mountains, and then leave Nat with strangers for the first time. Nat was eager about camp, but this unfortunately translated to an escalation in his most difficult behaviors. Throughout June he was nearly unmanageable. Things hit bottom when, during one of Nat's tantrums, my youngest, Ben, screamed, "When you do that, it makes me want to die!" Right then I almost scrapped the trip, and I even started to think about sending Nat to residential school, because clearly Ben needed some relief. This dynamic didn't seem healthy for either one of them.

But I persevered with our plans, and Ned was OK with this, too, as we went over all the potential problems and our proposed solutions to them, such as long lines at the airport (we would use a crisis story), tantrums on the airplane (our doctor prescribed a last-resort mild sedative for Nat), and so forth. We really wanted to try this trip.

On the day before we were to leave, Nat came home from school with a bursting backpack. Inside was a shiny laminated booklet illustrating his upcoming camp schedule of horse-back riding, hiking, rock climbing, water skiing, and rafting; a carefully worded daily calendar of the week; and photos of his friends and teachers to take with him. This was the mother of all crisis stories! I was nearly in tears when I called his teacher to thank her. As Nat enthusiastically leafed though his stuff, I felt a slight bubble of hope start to grow.

As these things usually go, the anticipation was far worse than the event itself, both for Nat and for us. Despite long security lines at the airport, the plane ride to Colorado was a breeze. Nat was uncharacteristically calm. By the time we got him to his camp, he was focused and grinning, leaving me no doubt as to how he would feel there. The place was woodsy, well staffed, and warm.

When we drove off without Nat, I felt both heavy and light at the same time. We were going to be without him for a week. Was it OK to leave him? The question rang through my head, but it didn't have the power to weigh me down. It was OK. It was just different. Perhaps I could have used my own crisis story! In any case, we settled into our new way of feeling—so strangely light—and set off on our Colorado adventure.

Even though Ned grumbled about the treacherous mountain passes he had to navigate, it felt like a blissful luxury to be able to think about nothing but the roads we were on, or to yell at Ben to look up from his Game Boy once in a while. Our five days stretched deliciously before us, under that impossibly wide, sparkling Colorado sky.

And so it was, a calm and wonderful week of exploring impulsively, planning very little—a rare treat for this autism family. We hiked, swam, lazed around, and ate a lot. All the daily reports from camp were excellent. No arm biting or tantrums; well, just once, but it was minor—and justified. Someone had forgotten Nat's socks, or something like that.

The end of the week brought us back to the camp in Aspen, refreshed and relaxed. I was ravenous to see Nat again. We all were, but Nat was nowhere in sight. "Keep watching the trees," a counselor told us. The trees? A few moments later, a rustling sound, and then, suspended on rope from a zipline, Nat came sailing through the trees with a hardhat on his head and a smile on his face.

On the ground again, he draped his arms heavily around me and we stood quietly with his head bent to my shoulder. I breathed in the sunbaked smell of his skin. *My darling. I'm so proud of you. I missed you so much,* I thought. My heart was thick in my throat.

We were going home together, but the separation had been so peaceful and yet also exhilarating. Our Colorado trip was a real learning experience for me about following through with my own goals, and honoring the family's need to grow and have fun—even if it meant taking new risks.

Putting our own needs in the picture can be a tall task when our lives are all about the kids, but it is manageable if we think about changing small things, bit by bit. Sometimes all we need is faith that we can handle whatever happens even if things don't end up OK—and then they do.

Ways to Have Fun with Your Kid

- If you're thinking big, such as a trip via plane, go all the way. Plan everything, down to the departure time. Many autism parents pay extra in order to be able to schedule the departures and arrivals that work best for their family's needs.

- If you think he'd enjoy it, try a sports camp—unless you really believe that he can't handle it—where you can participate or where he can go off and have fun without you, and you without him. But ask everything you need to ask in order to be as certain as possible of his success. See surfershealing.org or extremesports camp.org, or any inclusive camp that takes into account the needs of children on the spectrum, such as Camp Shriver: www.csde.umb.edu/shriver.html.

- Bring help if you can. Check out aupairinamerica .com, which might be more doable than you think. Or use respite money to cover a babysitter's plane ticket. (Many states have small amounts of funding set aside to provide respite for autism families. Ask your state's department of developmental services what is available.) Or beg a favorite family member to come along and you can owe him or her a favor later on.

- I found the following Web site wonderfully helpful

and full of resources on traveling with disabled children: holidayswithkids.com.au.

- Encourage family members to organize reunions in kid-friendly places and ask if you can get a break from your kids sometimes, with the family's help. Bring wine or barter something in exchange so that you won't feel beholden.

- If you aren't thinking big, try really small. One fun art or cooking project might not seem like much, but it always feels good to produce a little something with your children, even for fifteen minutes. Try a holiday-centered project, to help your child make connections with the holiday and fun or tasty treats. Disney's *FamilyFun* magazine has very good hands-on projects, both edible and artistic, to hold a child's interest.

- Reward small steps achieved, not only the end result. Small but meaningful rewards, such as animated praise or hugs or a series of tokens that end with a big treat, go a long way. The following site is very helpful for explaining how to use them: workingwithautism.info/rewardsystems.

- Check out this Web site, which has some commonsense ideas for helping yourself in difficult times: family-friendly-fun.com.

Also see what the CDC has to offer in terms of resources by checking out its Web site: cdc.gov. Search for autism resources there.

4

Me, Myself, and I
Why Self-Care Is Essential

IN THE LAST TEN YEARS, I have come to realize that my highs and lows have cycles nearly as predictable as the sunrise and sunset. Morning has always been my more energetic, upbeat time of day. Four in the afternoon is the definite nadir, the witching hour. I tend to need naps then, and my enthusiasm for my life drops along with my energy. This aspect of myself has given me a little insight into Nat, whose cycles of openness versus withdrawal (over the span of months, rather than days) seem to repeat fairly predictably as well. It took years of observation, conjecture, and hand wringing before Ned and I finally settled on an explanation akin to seasonal affective disorder. Nat becomes depressed and irritable at certain times of the year, and it seems directly tied to the intensity of the sun's warmth and light. For instance, his more withdrawn and anxious times of the year begin in late November when the daylight is briefest. He begins to be happier by early spring, and he is almost giddy on a daily basis in June and July.

Over the years I've also come to realize that some of the difficult times I have attributed to Nat's autism may actually have been the result of my own issues, namely, my struggles with depression. In a depressed state of mind, I see the happenings in my life through a gray and dreary lens. I wonder now if I was, at times, seeing Nat's behavior or affect clearly or if I was projecting my own hopelessness onto him. Or perhaps he was reacting to my mood. Knowing that this is very possible, that my withdrawal may have left him feeling insecure and unsettled, is difficult for me to bear.

My sense of guilt about how I may be negatively affecting or misperceiving Nat (and my other sons) frequently suffuses me, bleeding through even happy occasions sometimes. But this too I have begun to accept, just as I accept my allergies to cat hair and dust: my feelings of guilt are uncomfortable but not always there, and I can live with them, as long as I do what it takes to feel better.

These days, I don't just live with my depression. I have found ways to channel it into a different energy, shaking it up and molding it into something good, lemons into lemonade: I belly dance.

My metamorphosis usually starts around dinnertime, when Ned comes home from work. He toots his toylike Honda Civic horn, clamors up the stairs, and bellows, "Helloo!" and I feel like smiling for the first time in hours. Everything, even the very air around me, seems to shift subtly into a lighter, brighter version of itself. The dented black dining room table now looks pretty, like something out of a magazine, set with fluffy sage-colored floral napkins and shiny white plates. The old, dim gray stainless steel forks, a wedding present from twenty-five years ago, now seem to gleam under the light of our chandelier.

I have made it to dinner, and now I know I will most likely have a good evening. I have pushed through the difficult part, resisting going to bed at seven thirty or eight. Now I will find true joy: now I will belly dance. In the middle of this family of five and the chaos of after-dinner routines of homework and showers, with two teenage boys and one twelve-year-old, and a tired, overworked husband, I will put on a costume, Middle Eastern music, and dance until I am exhausted and drenched in sweat.

We eat fast, probably as most families do. Soon the dishes are cleared away, the counters wiped. Nat begins pacing the living room, waiting for it to be time to start his shower; Max shuffles off to the dining room or his bedroom to do homework; and Ben settles into the yellow loveseat to read. I rush upstairs and start to pull out my treasure trove of dance costumes from a plastic garment bag under the bed, and choose pink harem pants, a fuchsia skirt, a turquoise and silver hip scarf, and big earrings. I feel like a little girl raiding her dress-up box. Even though I am going nowhere but the living room, I assemble my costume carefully, as if it were a performance.

I emerge from my bedroom, bedecked and bejeweled from head to toe, my hip scarf jingling as I walk. Nat plunks down in the middle of the white living room couch because he loves the music—and maybe even the dancing. Max, my seventeen-year-old, sees me and makes no comment. Usually he goes up to his room at this point. I wonder as always if he is embarrassed by his belly-dancing mother. Probably. But it's also probably a good thing for him to see me doing something I love, I figure, even if it is not what his friends' mothers are doing with their free evenings. *Oh well, sorry, Max!* I think, but I'm not sorry, really. I have to do this; it is as strong a force as was my earlier despair. Where before I felt like if I didn't nap I would fall asleep in the middle of the kitchen floor, now the urge to dance is making me bounce around, hum Greek songs, and line my eyes like Cleopatra.

Ben, my twelve-year-old, asks me with a groan if I'm dancing again, and I say, "Yes," moving aside the coffee table with my knee and finding the right CD. I greet Nat and go about setting up a full-length mirror so that I can observe my technique. His eyes follow me as I move the mirror from its usual spot, something that would normally cause him to complain because he hates when things are out of place. But he says nothing, only settling himself in, his quiet self-stimulatory talk becoming more animated, an occasional grin flashing across his face. Sometimes he is my most enthusiastic audience.

I slip in the CD. I assume belly dancer's posture: back as long as possible, pelvis tucked, arms out but gently bent, thumbs and middle fingers almost touching. The music starts, and I already feel myself joining with it, my body straining to move. I am warm now, all poisonous feelings vanquished. I am a belly dancer.

Until Ben interrupts to ask, "Mom, do you have to do that every night?"

The answer is yes. Dancing is not only my antidote to depression, it is now a basic need. I discovered my love for belly dance one spring day a few years ago while watching a video with my teenage son, Max, of the Colombian pop singer Shakira, dancing to the song "Hips Don't Lie." Like Max, I was mesmerized by her movements and her athletic midsection. I wondered if she was actually using elements from belly dance, and I did some research and learned that, indeed, belly dancing had been her training.

I could not rid myself of the feeling of yearning I was having. I decided then and there that I wanted to learn how to belly dance, too. Why not, I thought? I can just take a night class, one night a week. If I don't like it, I won't continue. I moved quickly so that I would not lose my excitement or nerve. I signed up for a class taught by the adult education department of our school system and started a few weeks later.

The class was taught by a middle-aged woman herself, which immediately gave me more confidence. Also, I noticed that there were a variety of body types and ages in the class, not simply young and athletic women with perfect bodies. We giggled together about the movements the teacher showed us, so alien to anything else we had ever done. Many of us had been to classes at the gym or done other kinds of workouts, but this was different. Belly dance undid all of the cultural learning we had mastered about our bodies and how to hold them. Instead of keeping our bottoms tight and dignified, we were asked to shake them so that they felt as if they were falling off. Instead of sucking in our stomachs and trying to breathe anyway, we were asked to focus on each muscle group within our bellies and use them visibly.

The message I took from belly dancing was to celebrate the female body and all that it can do. The moves I learned in belly dance gave me more body confidence and a new way to get my husband's attention. I bought myself hip scarves, which led to my buying costumes and accessories to really create the right atmosphere. I downloaded exotic Arabic and Greek music onto my laptop. I turned my practices into performance opportunities, where I could both get a workout, get in touch with the "I am a Goddess" thing that comes with belly dancing, and put some sexy ideas into my (and Ned's) head.

Now belly dance is something I do regularly; it is my workout and my escape. It speaks to me on many different levels: it allows me to dress up in an exotic costume and play the role of someone else; it gives me a vehicle for seducing Ned, if I want to; it keeps me in touch with my sensual side, which can easily become submerged under the layers of activity that go with raising a special-needs child. Belly dancing isn't the point, however; what is important is what this activity does for me. Belly dancing gives me an identity and a space apart from the family me, the mom me. It is the way that I take time to care for myself and feed my spirit. We autism parents all need to find ways to do that.

NancyBea was a painter before she was an autism mom. We went to college together, and Ned and I still remember her hilarious and wise cartoons. Neither of us were surprised when she got an MFA and then later had art shows in Philadelphia and then New York City. She paints still lifes, landscapes, and people. Painting her children, particularly her autistic son, Henry, led her to develop a genre, which she calls Inclusion. Nancy described this concept as painting people with disabilities but not necessarily making the painting about the disability. There are paintings with disabled children in a swimming pool, or of her autistic son, Henry, stimming (engaging in self-stimulatory behavior, like hand-flapping). Her point was to paint people who are not normally subjects of portraits, calling attention to the more invisible people in art and in life. I asked her about how this concept began.

"I've always just painted my friends and family. I noticed that I started to paint Henry more often." At some point along the way, NancyBea discovered a disabled person in a historic painting, which ignited her imagination: "My brother sent me an article about a fifteenth-century painter who had two people with Down's syndrome in his painting—probably his own kids. I thought, 'Wow! They're just *there*, and nobody made a big deal out of it. Nobody had a name for it.' That's when I started thinking, 'Hmm, could I do that with disabilities, too?'" Thus her genre of Inclusion was born.

Painting is NancyBea's career, her vocation, her hobby, and her escape. But not *all* the time. She tries to pay attention to what she gets out of her painting, and what she needs at the time. "When I paint the still lifes, it is meditation for me. But when I do the genre of Inclusion painting, it is more emotional. It is *not* an escape. At a certain point, I get sick of painting about disability, so I don't do it all the time."

NancyBea says that it's important for her to know when painting helps her and when it does not. With autism in our lives, we have to know what works as an escape as well as what makes us feel that life is truly worth living. The latter can be big and "important," such as a career as an artist; or, used as an escape, it can be small and kind of crazy, like the way I belly dance in full costume in my living room.

Autism parents—if they are trying to find a better quality of life in the context of their struggle—have to come up with some solution of their own, whatever helps them feel like the individuals they are, and were, before becoming parents. Whatever helps, do it. That's one thing I've learned from those I've talked to and from my own experience.

My friend Ed from Ohio, who writes and performs poetry in his state, finds that poetry slams are a huge escape and release for him. Writing poems is also a way to explore his life with Neil and his feelings about living with autism. In fact, one of his poems, "After Birth," comparing Neil as a baby to a typically developing baby boy, is so powerful that it placed second in the 2009 Columbus (Ohio) Arts Festival.

Rebecca from Washington has found that scrapbooking is a creative way for her to plunge into her own world. "The process of scrapbooking is complex for me," she says, "since we are a special-needs family. For instance, what stories do I want to tell? What stories would I rather not remember?"

Rebecca says it's been easy for her to get into scrapbooking because there are so many resources. "There are many magazines dedicated to scrapbooking, and I struggle with this too. I see the pictures of other people's kids looking straight at the camera and smiling nicely. That is not our family's reality. Or I see the pages showing kids who are thrilled to be going back to school. On Noah's first day of school this year he was biting, throwing chairs, and hitting his teachers. How does one record that? How much should be glossed over?" Rebecca's solution is to create a private scrapbook that is just for her. "I tell the stories that I need to, for cathartic reasons, about myself and about my children. It's a process that I enjoy for the most part," she says.

Beth from Texas also enjoys making scrapbooks. "I feel happiest when I am creating," she says. "I am a huge scrapbooker. I am always working on photo albums. Both of the boys love to look at them, which is rewarding for me. I also like to sew and decorate. I'm just a creator." Beth says she also enjoys spending time with friends, wine tastings, going to dinner, shopping. "I also value my alone time," she says. "I am very comfortable alone, and I need that time to recharge so that I can be my best when Tanner is home."

Alastair, who lives in Cape Town, South Africa, wrote this to me about what he and his wife do for happiness outside of their parenting life: "My wife, Linda, has gone through a very difficult two years and required counseling and therapy. She's done very well with herself: she has given up smoking after twelve years of the habit and has found time to run every day. She is now running marathons! I have built a nursery and have a huge collection of bonsai trees, which I have started over the past two years after attending a few classes. Our son, Dylan, is always with me and is often referred to as 'Dad's shadow.' He loves the nursery and has picked up quickly on some aspects of the hobby. I hope that he will someday be able to sit for hours, as I do, and get lost in designing and maintaining these trees."

Sometimes we can find happiness in the simplest of activities: "I love to read," wrote Amy from Washington. "I buy way too many trashy magazines for a grown adult! I like *People* magazine because it has most of the famous people that I 'grew up' with." Just plain leaving for a little while also helps, as Amy described here: "I also love going on long drives with the radio turned *way* up, listening to some rock and roll and just shutting out the rest of the world for a bit." She says she also enjoys going for walks and chatting with girlfriends. For more long-term happiness, Amy is earning a degree in Early Childhood Education. "Going back to school is something that I have longed to do, I just never had a clear goal. Of course, now, those goals have been made crystal clear, and I am once again excited about each day."

Sometimes taking care of a living thing, in addition to kids, can be a metaphorical lifesaver as well. Bonnie from Michigan has a ten-year-old on the spectrum. "This is very weird and hard to justify," she says, "but I am really into having and caring for betta fish. I now have ten of them, and they each need a separate container, so it's a lot of work. But I like cleaning out their little homes, and they are very soothing to watch as they swim. Their coloring is gorgeous. They also act like they are interested in me, although I know they just want food. My family has threatened an intervention."

Eileen from Florida described her long journey to finding a way to be happy: "When I first had to accept the fact that my child had a serious disability, it was an extremely dark time. He was still a baby, only fifteen months old, when we took him to a toddler autism screening and my fears were confirmed. I was still breast-feeding him and in a weird way felt as if I had been diagnosed too, or as if we had both died or something. I felt very alienated from my husband and family, as if no one else 'got it,' or else they were minimizing it."

Eileen discovered motorcycling as her way of coping and creating balance. "When bike week came in March, for some reason I knew I had to go out on my husband's motorcycle with him. Previously I had absolutely no interest in doing this; he had taken me for a ride once and I was nervous and hated it. But now I knew that for my own sanity I needed to go out and do something that would force me to take my mind off things for a bit. Though I had always been such a Nervous Nellie about biking, now my fear seemed to be gone. My attitude became, 'If something bad's going to happen, it's just going to happen.' After all, my compulsively good and healthy habits didn't prevent my son from being autistic. That first ride was two-and-a-half years ago and since then my husband and I have logged thousands of miles together."

Eileen adds, "It is so much fun to play dress up each week, put on my leathers, a sexy top, my biggest earrings, and go for a ride along the ocean with several other bikers. We always wind up at a fabulous biker hangout hole-in-the-wall where we find amazingly interesting people to talk to. Seriously, I don't know how I would have gotten through the past couple of years without our beautiful black Road King. The together time with hubby is a big plus too! We are fortunate to live in an area that provides great riding weather year-round and has a strong biker community." There's a key word, *community*. The more I talked to people, the more that factor seemed to be the key to personal happiness, given the difficulties brought by autism.

Two of my blogger friends are Laura from Indiana and Alice from Texas. Both women gave me lists of what they do with their personal time to satisfy their needs to feel like a whole person, not defined by autism. I thought it was interesting to see how similar they were.

Alice's Fun List

- Eat chocolate and occasionally drink wine
- Take walks in pretty places
- Yoga (very easy yoga)
- Read good novels
- Talk to old friends or my sisters on the phone
- Watch *The View* (now that kids are in preschool, yay)
- Take a long hot shower
- Watch sappy chick flicks

Laura's Fun List

- Eat chocolate
- Run, bike
- Take walks
- Play tennis
- Read
- Call my sisters, call a friend
- Play online Scrabble
- Watch reality TV, *The Office,* and *Seinfeld* reruns
- Hang out with my typical

- Buy myself things at Target
- Go out with my husband to restaurant, then bookstore
- Drink strong coffee or tea
- boy (he reminds me that I'm not a refrigerator mother!)
- SHOP
- Take my autistic son to his favorite places because his joy is so reassuring
- Make love to my husband
- Read your blog
- Go to my special-needs mom group
- Pray
- Listen to my iPod
- Play with my cats

It is not shameful to do things for yourself, and to want to be the star sometimes. It is not being selfish; it is being self-caring. What's more, it is absolutely imperative; not just because we'll be better mothers after we've been good to ourselves, but because we need to do this to be full human beings. Our children are a part of us, but they are not all of us. We don't have to feel guilty about putting them aside for a while thinking only about ourselves. But parents of special-needs kids forget that. They may feel subconsciously responsible for their child's issues. We may have a lot of guilt about our child's struggles. We feel so much a part of our children that we are heavily burdened by anything that happens to them. That is a lot to carry around.

This means that we parents with disabled kids have to work even harder to keep ourselves from disappearing into our children's lives, from becoming part of the background or the furniture. I have to fight the guilt that crops up out of nowhere and think about myself, my needs. I have to carve out meaningful moments, and commit to myself in doing so, in every way possible: with pleasurable activities, large or small.

In remembering to take care of ourselves, something as seemingly mundane as appearance can be an important issue. Julie from Massachusetts says, "I've always struggled with weight issues and for the past couple of years I've been taking antidepressants, which became a necessity for me after both of my PDD kids were diagnosed. I just couldn't handle it and went to some very dark places. SSRIs such as Prozac can cause people to gain weight, and after my dosage was increased last year, I've put on twenty-five pounds and am struggling mightily to take it off. It sucks, frankly. But I'm afraid to go off the medicine, or even alter the prescription, because of the stress of dealing with this wonderful but very high-maintenance family." Julie stresses that "the way I've helped myself most is by getting into therapy and taking an antidepressant."

I could relate to what Julie said, because I have been struggling for a few years with the same problem, give or take a few pounds. And the more stuck I feel in my weight, the worse I feel, which leads to more unhealthy eating—we all know that cycle. The premium we put on looking good is hard to live up to, especially in the context of raising a child with special needs.

According to a recent issue of *Vogue,* I shouldn't be wearing my hair long anymore. Apparently once you hit your mid-forties, hair past your collarbone is ridiculous, laughable. But I'm going to fight for my right to wear my hair long at age forty-seven, or sport a miniskirt, carry a few extra pounds, or whatever I want. If a certain fashion choice gives me a little happiness, then it *must* be done.

Eileen, my biker-chick friend, told me, "I don't spend a lot of time on my appearance. The other day my teenage daughter saw the lipstick I use—there was nothing left to it. She said, 'Mom, go get new lipstick!' That struck me as so funny, that I let my lipstick get like that, a concave glimpse of pink, without it even occurring to me to go get a new one. In my life right now that seems way too self-indulgent! The biggest thing I do for myself is eat right, watch my figure, and stay slim. I get my hair cut and highlighted twice a year. That's about it!"

Amy from Washington told me about her own self-care regimen, which makes a difference in her outlook. "I get up for work way earlier than my hubby deems 'necessary,' but I need time to wake up and get a clear head. I shower every day, that is a *must* for me. I function better and can take on the world when I am clean-smelling!" Although showering may seem like nothing special, there are so many moms who feel like it's a miracle if they get a shower in every day! Basic hygiene should not become optional. Making time for this basic, truly necessary practice is very important in terms of feeling good about yourself and just plain starting your day refreshed.

Susan from Massachusetts reminded me that spiritual grounding can be an important aspect of self-care: "I go to yoga class and to a Zen meditation class once a week. In addition I try to meditate daily for at least twenty minutes and do yoga three times a week at home, but I mostly fail at this part because of time constraints and/or laziness. The two classes each week, though, truly save my sanity." Alastair from South Africa told me that his son's autism brought him a new faith in God: "I have never been close to God or had much faith, but since Dylan was brought into our lives, I have found my faith, and it gives me a lot of peace. Faith is a gift Dylan has given me."

For autism parents, physical exercise can be as important as spiritual rejuvenation. "Exercise is some thing that makes me feel good about myself," Amy said along these same lines. "I feel like I've accomplished something when I feel sweat pouring down my face and can say 'I just ran two miles,' or when I can look at the elliptical machine and see that I have burned four hundred calories." Exhausting exercise followed by a hot shower can revitalize your spirit like few other things.

Tips and Strategies for Taking Care of Ourselves

- For inspiration on the subject of loving yourself and your body, read *The Joy Diet* by Martha Beck. Or take a look at some postings at firstourselves.com, a Web site dedicated to self-care for women. For a slightly lighter take, read "10 Steps to Feeling Good Naked," from *O* magazine (you can find this article by searching the title at the magazine link at oprah.com).

- Therapy or counseling may be helpful to you, as it has been for me and so many other autism moms. Find a therapist by asking your primary care doctor for a recommendation, or ask a friend. If finances are an issue, some psychologists have sliding scales, and some towns and cities also have mental health centers that offer counseling at reduced rates.

- Yoga, exercise, and meditation can be lifesavers. If you're interested in meditation, check out Mindfulness-Based Stress Reduction (MBSR) online. This is a simple form of meditation practice, developed by Jon Kabat-Zinn, that promotes health and well-being. (MBSR classes are taught around the country.) For research-based information on the benefits of meditation, go to the Mayo Clinic Web site and search "meditation." If you can't get to a class, try an introductory book-and-audio program such as *Quiet Mind: A Beginner's Guide to Meditation* edited by Susan Piver.

- Consider getting back in touch with your faith, or exploring a spiritual tradition you've always been interested in. For some parents, an active spiritual life adds balance, comfort, and grounding.

- How do you feel about the way you look? Think about it. This is not as superficial an issue as it might seem:

how we feel about our appearance can help or harm our outlook on life. Neglecting our appearance is the easiest thing to do as a parent, especially during difficult times, but for most of us that only makes us feel worse. So do what you can, right away, to make yourself feel better in this department. Whether it's buying a new tube of lipstick, like Eileen, just taking the time to brush your hair, or going to a salon—it feels good! (If you can't get to the salon, maybe your partner would wash your hair for you. The physical contact is playful and fun for you both.) Or ask your child to play with your hair. It's fun for both of you. You can even do some educational role-playing, but the truth is, the touch of little fingers on your scalp is heavenly.

- Regarding weight issues: Don't crash-diet or do anything self-hating or self-defeating! (I guess I should learn how to take my own advice.) Instead, put together a special outfit that makes you feel good. Clothing problems? Buy more clothes! If I'm overweight, I buy one or two new things in a bigger size so that I have something good to put on—but don't you dare call them "fat clothes." And if my weight is good, I buy a new piece that will jazz up what I have, even if it's just earrings, or if I'm lucky, a new pair of pants or shoes. Having something to look forward to wearing is very special and lots of fun.

- Check out *MomSpa: 75 Relaxing Ways to Pamper a Mother's Mind, Body and Soul,* by Jennifer Sander.

MOVING FROM STRUGGLING PARENT
TO BALANCED HUMAN BEING

Sometimes I find it really difficult to take an afternoon off, or just an hour off, even when it is practically handed to me tied up in a bow. I cannot always make the transition to tending to my own happiness. It is not easy for me to shift seamlessly from one mode of being to another. Especially during a crisis time, my friendships often fade, and when it comes time for a get-together, it is not unusual for me to find myself reluctant to go. Why? I still don't understand that fully.

This kind of self-defeating behavior is surely the road to hell. Maybe I'm like Nat in the sense that I have trouble transitioning, in this case, from my drudgery at home to the freedom of an evening out with a friend. Maybe it's because the hell we are used to is preferable to the unknown and new? When I am down in the inferno, right when I need a break most is when I am most likely to cancel an outing with a friend at the last minute.

In these situations, it's good for me to have a little reminder pinned to the fridge or somewhere prominent that says "You should go. You need this. It will be fun." Or I ask my husband to push me out the door for a night out. But sometimes I have that inexplicable reluctance, or sometimes I feel selfish leaving, and the guilt suffuses me and threatens to spoil the fun. In times like these, I find it is best to pare down the outing to a bearable amount of time, maybe to a cup of coffee, something that only takes an hour.

Or sometimes I find a way to transition to a pleasurable

outing by turning to one of my "Keys to the Universe." Some time ago I realized that there were some simple activities and products that always, always worked for me, every time. They are not big-deal items, but are rather everyday things that granted a small bit of satisfaction right when I needed it. Sometimes using one of these is all it takes for me to feel human again and to get me out the door.

Some "Keys to the Universe"
(Small Pleasures That Make a Big Difference)

- Plunge into a hobby for a brief moment. For example, I take a few minutes and go to bhuz.com to connect with the international belly dance community (for news and a great swap meet). I might decide to buy a new belly dance accessory: a hip scarf, veil, CD, or finger cymbals, to keep my interest alive. Acquiring any small item that is about your hobby works wonders for taking you out of a lousy moment and into a better one.

- Go out to a nice dinner with a close friend. For me, it's dinner with one of my best girlfriends (the ones who laugh at all my stupid jokes), complete with a pomegranate martini and tuna tataki rolls. Even just once or twice a year, this is a great boost. In a pinch, grabbing a coffee together will do. Sometimes if I can't get out

---

of the house, I even brew a pot and call someone, and drink it "with" them for a nice break.

- Challenge yourself physically. I like taking a bike ride where there's lots of hills on which to pound out my emotions. In bad weather, a StairMaster and iPod will do; at night, I belly dance.

- Do something that stimulates your intellect—exercise your mind. I make a thorough lesson plan for the English course I teach at a nearby college or do a crossword puzzle.

- Join a club or interest group. My writers' group is basically a support group. They understand the highs and lows of this job. Now there are meetups you can join wherever you live, and get together with others who enjoy the same things. Go to meetup.com to find such a group for your interests.

- Do something small and quick that makes you feel good about your appearance. For me it's L'Oréal self-tanning lotion—a slight tan makes me feel like I've been on a vacation.

- Indulge in a treat, for example, a Cadbury Chocolate Creme Egg. When I allow myself this, it is the best food on earth, with "real" egg yolk inside made of gushy sweet vanilla cream. A mouthful of delight.

- Enjoy a glass of something tasty. Every once in a while, I pour myself one perfect glass of wine while I make dinner, to soften my head a little bit. Even if I'm making chicken nuggets and noodles, I feel like a sophisticated chef with my pretty wine glass on the counter. Fantasy goes a long way in an otherwise harried life. (But don't overdo it with wine or liquor. If you have a history of dependence on alcohol, use a different "key"! A hot chocolate, instant lemonade, or fruity iced tea can work too.)

- Enjoy the beauty of nature. I always get a lift from getting flowers, any flowers, especially pink roses and blue delphinium. I buy them for myself at the supermarket if need be. Taking a walk in a beautiful spot with a friend or by yourself can also be very restoring.

- Put on some music. A song or a symphony, we all have a favorite piece that will fill us with joy and energy. If you play an instrument, take it out, even if you think you are not in the mood. The immediacy of the sounds under your fingers and into your ears are magical, but sometimes we forget. Or find a live performance and experience the music all around you.

- Visiting a Web site that helps you with your overall philosophy of life may be just what you need. For example, see happiness-project.com.

5

Improving Our Love Lives
Yes, That's Important, Too!

HOW DO TWO PEOPLE who are so many things to each other (friend, partner, diaper changer, breadwinner, bread baker, autism teammate) switch gears and go back to being lovers? It is tough in any kind of family, but with autism in the mix, the intimacy situation between spouses can be an even bigger challenge. We're worried about making it to various appointments and are dealing with the constant educational and therapeutic issues that crop up—everything from learning yet again that a speech therapy session in school did not happen to wondering how to toilet train, to getting a child to sleep the whole night or to stop biting.

My friend NancyBea put it this way: "We are not weird if we're not having sex. It should be OK to admit that with autism in the family it's really hard to have *any* kind of sex life."

Of course it's not weird if autism parents stop having sex, but it's also true that we don't have to put this aspect of our lives on hold either. Most of us don't want to disconnect sexually from our partners, but how do we prevent it, with such a lot on our plates? We all know that a person's sex drive can be buried under family needs, long work hours, health and self-esteem issues, even boredom. We also know that autism can compound any of the above. However, once begun, sex is always worth the effort. It is so oddly ironic that now, married and older, we think of sex as something to work at, just as, when we're young, it takes will-power not to do it! Nevertheless, I do know that sex is and will always be a key ingredient to my personal happiness, particularly in a long-term relationship such as a marriage. But knowing something and feeling it do not always go hand in hand, especially with something as complex as sexuality, where there can be many disconnects between what you want in your mind and heart and what your body can do.

The psychologists and autism moms I contacted confirmed that most of us are focused on just getting through the day. In our harried lives, it is so easy just to let sexuality go. Dr. Sharon Waller, a clinical psychologist in Brookline, Massachusetts, says, "In my therapy sessions with autism moms, it's hard to get them to focus on themselves. The way they use the time we have together is to talk about their child. Their therapy is primarily about getting validation and support for their decisions related to treatment options for their child, the IEP process [Individualized Education Program], and addressing behavioral challenges in their children. When they do refer to their marriages, they might say in passing, 'We never have sex anymore.'"

Dr. Waller points out that having children often strains a marriage, whether the children have special needs or not. "The research points to a decline in marital satisfaction once children arrive," she says. However, the difference autism makes is in the frequency and intensity of the problems. When raising an autistic child, challenges crop up again and again, often unpredictably.

Many autism parents want to improve their love lives, but are not sure how they can. Kristina from North Carolina told me that the flesh might indeed be willing, but the spirit is weak—or just plain exhausted. "I still find sex with my husband very enjoyable," she says, "and every time we have sex I find myself thinking, *Why don't we do this more often?* Then it hits me, we're both so damned tired all the time, that's why. We're constantly chasing our tails, trying to catch up with just the regular day-to-day duties of being homeowners, parents, and professionals. At the end of the day, when we can finally slow down long enough to take a breath, there's simply nothing left to give most of the time."

Kristina adds, "Yes, I realize that parents of typically developing children are tired as well. However, even my close friends with typical kids acknowledge that my husband and I are exhausted to a degree that goes beyond 'normal' parental exhaustion. On top of the ordinary demands of day-to-day parenting, we have to manage excessive tantrums, aggressive behavior, stimming, and all the therapies. Added to that, most auties I know don't sleep! It all adds up to profound exhaustion—mental, physical, and emotional."

We owe it to ourselves to make sure that there's room for intimacy in our lives. No matter what we are up against, love is a basic human need, necessary for our personal nourishment. It is indeed possible to honor this need, but in order to do so, we have to acknowledge that it is really OK , and not selfish, to want this. So how can people dealing with autism in their lives allow themselves personal pleasure and connection, given their busy, demanding, and stressful lives?

The more I asked around, gently, about marital happiness and thought about the frustrated responses I got, the more I realized that the only way to approach these dilemmas at all is to start with small, simple goals. Ned has often said to me, "If you want to make a change, start with one easy thing today." In other words, set yourself up for success. If we go around thinking of ourselves as "never having sex," and if we go right to "Oh, just forget it," then that door will probably stay closed longer than it has to.

Dr. Waller tells me that some of her patients have been able to make some headway by making one small change: a commitment to a set bedtime for the children. With one family in particular, the problem was a lack of a consistent bedtime routine, compounded by the child's need for the parent to be in the room until she fell asleep. "This mother did not leave the child's room until after ten P.M.," says Dr. Waller, "and by that time she was ready to go to sleep herself. This type of scenario precludes any time alone with her husband." So this couple has started creating a structured bedtime routine that frees up the mother earlier in the evening. Dr. Waller adds, "This means not getting off track with dinner, showers, computer time, and so on. Try to be done at a reasonable time given your child's age." Books such as Mary Sheedy Kurcinka's *Sleepless in America* can help by giving you some ideas regarding bedtime routines, relaxation techniques, and promoting better sleep habits. However, since Kurcinka recommends short massages at bedtime, it might be a good idea to check with an occupational therapist about whether massage should be used to help your autistic child relax, since sensory issues are so often a challenge with autism.

Kevin, an autism dad and fellow blogger living in the U.K., believes firmly in keeping the boundaries in terms of kid time versus adult time: "We make sure our kids know they are loved, too, just the way they are. But when they're in bed, it's our time to indulge each other." Another autism dad, Alastair from Cape Town, South Africa, has a similar playful attitude toward his private life with his wife, Linda: "Linda likes to play Texas Hold'em online. I attend to my collection of bonsai trees. But as often as we can, we play with each other." Although Alastair did not mention if "often" was often enough, he certainly sounded like a happily married person on the telephone and in his e-mail responses.

If the issue is not about kids' bedtime demands, but about time in general, some creative, calculated risk taking may be in order. Provided all the other elements are in place (namely, that you and your spouse both *want* to connect sexually, but that time alone is the main issue), a certain amount of sneaking around may be necessary. Zoe, an autism mom living in

Maryland, told me how she manages to make things happen for her and her husband, even when their son, Hayden, is in a particularly difficult phase. "In late April, while Hayden was exhibiting his most dangerous self-injuring behaviors, I still sent him to school, because it was on a day when my younger son (who is homeschooled) was going to be out for a few hours. This meant that my husband (who works from home) and I could have sex."

Zoe continues, "As stressed as I was about Hayden's mental state, I knew I needed to take care of myself. Hayden will not go to bed at night without me, and it would take hours of waiting for him to go to sleep before I could even consider having sex. So, selfishly, I sent him to school, having given him Ativan (which didn't help), and tried to forget about him for thirty minutes while my husband and I connected. I knew my problem would still be waiting for me afterward, and somehow I was able to put it out of my head for a short time." Although Zoe was very uncomfortable with using medication to help calm Hayden so that she could have some time with her husband, she also knows that she is human and has a basic human need for connection. Zoe explains that she wasn't always able to be as self-caring as this. "I don't know what changed in me," she says, "but I've suddenly come to the realization that my husband and I need and deserve our time together. We've been married eighteen years."

Some couples use the sneaky element to enhance their enjoyment of each other. Kaija, an autism mom I met in South Dakota, told me, "We just take it when we can get it! We'll sneak away while Aaron's watching a movie, or meet at home for 'lunch' during the week. Once in a while we'll sneak away for a night or two, or a long weekend away. And we take a yearly trip to Mexico to reconnect and act like young, crazy lovers."

I almost wish that time were the issue for Ned and me, but our difficulty is more about moving ourselves across that line between friendship and sex. Ned and I have a somewhat complicated history of having been friends for a long time before we very cautiously moved into romance and marriage. So for us, though we've been married for more than twenty-five years, it is far too easy to slip back into being friends, and to let our sex life get lost in the business of running our household and managing our boys, and to see each other as comrades. Living in friend mode does not easily segue into passion mode—unless you both know how to use your friendship to your advantage.

FANNING THE FLAMES

Over the years Ned and I have figured out how to move back and forth from the roles of Mommy and Daddy to Ned and Sue. The way we do that is first and foremost to agree that our own relationship, apart from our relationships with our children, is a top priority. This goes beyond making a commitment to each other, the way we did when we got married. Now, after more than twenty-five years together, we make a conscious effort to maintain the feeling of being special to each other.

Our efforts are not ceremonious or grand; it's almost never about candlelight or soft music. Keeping each other special requires directing a sort of mental energy toward the other. Ned and I make the effort to keep each other in our minds, allowing in small daydreams of one passionate evening during a vacation or even just recalling a sensual image. If I find my thoughts wandering to Ned during a lull in the day, I let them linger there, calling to mind my favorite things: his face, or strong arms, or deep, male voice. This way, he suddenly stands apart from my mundane activities, special and unique to everything else in my life. Sometimes that's all it takes to revive a warm—or even a hot—connection. Perhaps each of us just has to find that one thing about their mate that simply turns us on. We have to let ourselves think this way; we have to give ourselves that permission to indulge our needs and desires with our partner.

For Kaija, too, just *allowing* herself to think of her partner in a sexual way has been a kind of revelation. "After Aaron was born, sex was almost nonexistent," she says. "His demands on me were relentless. Sex felt like a chore, one more thing I had to do to make someone other than me happy. It was just too hard, or too late, or too exhausting, too everything. But one day about three years ago, I woke up and literally craved my husband's touch. I wanted his undivided affection and his way of wanting and needing me like no one else in my life can. I suddenly realized he wasn't someone that I had to take care of, or teach, or feed. I just had to let him in. He only wanted me for me, nothing else, and I had pushed him and us aside and given myself totally over to the care of our son."

Kevin and his wife, Naomi, also crave each other's company, and they keep this feeling going by maintaining an element of spontaneity when possible: "We are pretty adventurous and love to do things that we know please the other," he says. "Having 'us' time is not easy, and we have come to a slow accommodation with the world. We get little to no opportunity to go out for meals or evenings out, so we try and do small, spontaneous things for each other. For example, I might order a book that Naomi wants and surprise her with it or bring back a bunch of flowers. Something, anything, that lets the other person know that they are valued beyond their role as parent."

Kevin offers this advice: "As individuals, each partner must feel able to nurture herself or himself in whatever ways they need; some people like to work out at a gym, take a walk, do some gardening, read fiction, listen to music, take a bath—whatever is relaxing for that person. As a couple, you can decide together to take a little time with each other—go for a walk, share a cup of tea or a glass of wine, watch a favorite movie, go for a drive. Whatever helps you to reenergize, even a little bit, and nurture yourselves."

Michael, a dad from Massachusetts, feels that marital connection is all about simplicity. "A little bit can go a long way," he says. "It doesn't have to be a two-week vacation. It can be a walk with your spouse, a movie. An afternoon off can be a big deal."

Bonnie from Michigan has a great and simple way of spending time with her husband that does not involve sex or leaving the house, but does make them feel good together: "I love doing this silly workout called Turbo Jam." (See turbo jam.com.) "It's a combination of dance and kick boxing, and the music is crazy and the instructor is overly energetic and fun. I just feel powerful, cool, and young when I do it. My knees tell me different afterward, but it's a small price to pay. Better still, my hubby actually does it with me occasionally, which is nice!" Anything our spouses can do with us is a bonus, of course, because having fun together almost always will mean a stronger marriage.

Similar to Bonnie, NancyBea has found that connecting over adult activities can help your marriage. NancyBea and her husband, Paul, rarely go out at all just the two of them—on fancy dinner dates or things like that. "But when we do go out, we like to go to dinner parties with lots of conversation. Sometimes it's easier being in a group of adults. Or we like having people over who've known Henry for a long time and just remain unfazed if he walks in wearing nothing but his boxers."

NancyBea's sense of humor about her family life seems to keep her and Paul connected. Humor is one of the basic elements that also helps Ned and me. Usually through laughing at ourselves, even at difficult, tense moments, we continue to feel like ourselves and not like slaves to the demands of disability. Having our own private jokes, even about the kids, is a way that we ease the consuming struggle of family life with disability.

The other night Ned and I were able to bond over an odd but funny Chinese dinner with Nat, and the evening was a little like Chinese food: sweet and sour. Both Max and Ben, our two typical kids, went to sleep over at friends' houses, so Ned and I were home alone with Nat. We decided to go out to a restaurant we would not usually go to with all five of us, because we knew that Nat, although autistic, is the most mature and least picky eater of the three boys, and would eat well anywhere.

We drove around and around looking for parking, which in our urban town can be enough to dampen one's enthusiasm. I could just feel Nat becoming more tense with each disappointment. He hates failed parking attempts, and he can feel the tension between us as we discuss what to do. This makes him anxious. Our dialogue went something like this:

NED: Oh, there's one, she's leaving!

SUSAN: No, Ned, that's not a legal spot!

NED: Oh, sorry.

SUSAN: Jeez, who are they honking at?

(Nat, in the backseat, is bouncing his leg up and down and muttering more and more loudly.)

SUSAN: Natty, it's OK. Hey, what about that spot? Can I get to it from here?

NED: Yeah, but—d'oh, that person just took it.

SUSAN: This time I'll drive around and go left. I have a little secret parking area.

NED: Oh, look at this, clever!

SUSAN: See? Good parking karma.

SUSAN: (upon exiting car) Nat, you were very calm while we were parking. Good work!

NED: Yeah. Natty, hold my hand.

(Nat, still anxious, pinches and scratches Ned's hands.)

NED: Nat, calm hands! Nat, we won't go into the restaurant if you pinch.

NAT: Go restaurant.

NED: Then don't pinch.

NAT: No pinch. Go restaurant.

Ned and I looked at each other, shrugged, and hoped for the best. It was the look we exchanged that is most important here; it turned the experience into something we were in together. It gave us a tiny bit of perspective then and there, which is very valuable for bonding.

Once inside the restaurant, we sat at a window booth, which always makes me happy. Ned ordered spareribs for us to share, which I thought I wouldn't like, but, wow, I was wrong. After having about five little pieces, I discovered the honey-colored sauce beneath the pile. No wonder.

Ned said, smiling at me, "See? Pigs taste good." I laughed, because Ned says this sometimes, to "prove" to me that I should cook more pork. (Shared jokes like "Pigs taste good" is a way of increasing intimacy, by building our couple culture, our sense of our history together.)

I said, sighing, but smiling, "Yes, they certainly do."

It was a bit of a struggle getting Nat to try the spareribs, but neither Ned nor I would give up, because we knew he would love them. Finally, I put a little greasy pink chunk on his plate and said, "Nat, it's like bacon. It's sweet, too. You'll like it. Just try it." He gingerly poked at it and touched it to his tongue, and then, of course, he was completely blown away.

Ned and I continued to talk about whatever we wanted to, not afraid of kid interruptions. (Nat never interrupts; he barely initiates any conversation at all.) We talked, among other things, about our sex life, using subtle code language and innuendo, so that Nat would remain in the dark. This would never have worked if our next oldest son, Max, had been there, so it was a lot of fun and kind of challenging trying to keep such a secretive conversation going. Nat continued to eat and seemed very absorbed with his spareribs.

A semipeaceful, enjoyable dinner with my husband—and my nearly grown autistic son. Not exactly how I pictured a Saturday night out, way back when, but back then, what did I know? I didn't even realize that pigs taste good.

It's important for autism parents to figure out, on-the-go, how to grab a little couple fun and connect with each other, even in the midst of a tense situation. Whenever things get difficult with your child, try to step back and realize that whatever is going on right now will pass. I have a friend who tells herself, "Pretend I'm watching a sitcom," and it helps her laugh at what's going on at the moment.

A lot of autism parents can even bond over a child's

difficult behavior by forming a united front together. Once your child is under control, acknowledge what you have done and let that good feeling in. This sounds simple, but you may be surprised how infrequently you do it. Turn to your spouse and share it somehow, perhaps with a wink or a small joke, or lean over and give him a tiny kiss. (If he says, "What?" You can smile enigmatically and say, "What what?" Keep the moment and the mystery going. This is how you begin to amass good moments together.) Once this tense moment is in the past, you can remind each other of it in a lighthearted way and strengthen your connection.

Of course there are times when connection just isn't happening for Ned and me, so we have each gone for counseling at one time or another to help us understand how we can bridge the gaps between us and grow as a couple and as individuals. It has been essential for us to realize that we both need help dealing with autism's challenges. Dr. Cindy Ariel, a family psychologist in Philadelphia, says, "Women have traditionally been the emotional gatekeepers of the family and as such they have been the ones to seek help for themselves, their marriage, or their children." Women do seem to make the initial phone call to a therapist or professional more often than men. However, moms are by no means the only ones who are distressed or who care to work toward the emotional well-being of their marriage and their children. Fathers may handle the emotional piece differently, but given support, encouragement, and enough free time (around their work schedules), they are often very willing participants.

BUBBLES

Sometimes when things are at a low point with Nat, I just sit there staring, feeling the pain wash over me. Every now and then, Ned notices this and invites me to come lean against him. He silently puts his arm around me. Ned refers to moments like these as a tiny bubble, his concept of a small protective space you create alone or with your spouse that buffers you for an instant from everything that is upsetting you. "Bubbles" don't solve anything. They will not make you into a happy person if you suffer from depression, and they will not change an unhappy marriage into a happy one. Bubbles will not stop your child from having a tantrum, and they will not pay the therapy bills, but they are tremendously important because they are instant de-stressors. They are the quiet, deep breaths you draw to help steel yourself for the next tough time. Bubbles are necessary every single day, because they buffer us from the constant pressures and demands we feel. They are the spaces between accomplishing something "important." They are the simple moments of just being, of inner strengthening, and they are essential.

We autism parents should be doing everything available to us for living whole lives. Too many parents with special-needs kids see themselves as the background, the facilitator, the supporting cast, the therapist, rather than the star of the show. They feel guilty about taking time for themselves.

Parents need to know that they have the right to place their own needs in the picture, too. But they have to be creative and open-minded about how to do this, since it is not always possible to be just the two of you alone. It may not be possible to go out on any sort of date at the moment. In that case, we can try escaping without going anywhere. We have to try to find fun in tiny bursts of time, in less-than-perfect circumstances, such as winking at each other across a chaotic, crowded room, two ships passing in the night. We can bond over just a small thing, a joke perhaps. We can even bond by bickering with each other! Sometimes the mental stimulation creates positive sparks. I have found that anything that has happened in the family, no matter what it is—anything that you have survived as a couple—can and should become grist for your couple culture and ensuing passion, as long as it is truly in the past. It all starts with letting yourself be that sexual adult that you used to be, and then taking just a little time to figure out how you and your partner can go back there. That side of you is still there, underneath the ABA charts and the IEP meetings and the worry. You will probably find that you enjoy the escape while you are rediscovering the two of you.

Reviving Intimacy

- Though intimacy can be difficult with autism in the family, it is worth the effort! For useful tips, check out this Web site: life.familyeducation.com and search for the article called "Obstacles to a Great Sex Life."

- Remember that intimacy should be unique to the two of you. It doesn't always have to be candles, Mozart, or even sex. See: marriage.about.com/cs/sex/a/marriage sex.htm, which describes different kinds of couples and what they can do to remain on good intimate terms.

- You might only need that "bubble" to start bringing it all back. Keep your expectations reasonable. Any time together that is sweet and calm is worthwhile. Remember, it's just a bubble, a tiny fix; don't expect the world to change (otherwise Ned would have called it a tsunami instead of a bubble).

- When you make special time to be together, no kids allowed! Talk about other things—something you just read, something you're interested in. Or discuss favorites (vacations you've taken, movies you've seen). Try guessing each other's favorites.

- Be young again. Flirt with and tease your husband. Make subtle dirty jokes. Send sexy e-mails, leave breathy messages in his voice mail (nothing that will get you or him fired!). This might sound like a cliché, but remember, we're trying to rediscover that spark that is still there somewhere, hidden under too-comfy clothes, trips to occupational therapy, and arguments about bills.

- It's all in your head. Intimacy is a state of mind. Even if the kids are swarming around you, make eye contact with your husband and share a moment: a wink, a smile, a joke whispered. If you do this regularly, you might start to feel something growing between you.

- Get some rest. Take a page from Kristina's book: "We take turns sleeping in on the weekends, and I am able to take naps, which is a *huge* boost. Just getting that sorely needed rest gives you a second wind and a better outlook, which simply isn't possible during the week."

- Remind yourself that you and your spouse are in it together—no nagging! There's helpful information on conflict resolution—such as getting to the bottom of an argument or just how to talk and listen—for couples at the BBC Web site bbc.co.uk/relationships/couples/comm_index.shtml.

- Take a look at *Communication Miracles for Couples*, by Jonathan Robinson, and *Why Can't You Read My Mind? Overcoming the 9 Toxic Thought Patterns That Get in the Way of a Loving Relationship* by Jeffrey Bernstein and Susan Magee, for more tips on easy and effective relationship-enhancing strategies.

6

Moving beyond "You and Me against the World"

Getting Help from Others

A RECURRING MEMORY I have goes like this: I'm sitting in the sandbox with three-year-old Nat. Babies are seated nearby, stuffed sausagelike into their pastel clothes, short legs splayed outward for balance. Mothers and younger, ponytailed nannies squat on the granite edges of the sandbox or sit in conversation on the benches nearby.

I'm trying not to pay much attention to the obvious pleasure around me, because I am not a part of it. I am focused on Nat, who digs his fingers into the sand, down into the deeper, moist parts, and grabs onto two big clumps. I know what's coming next, yet I watch mesmerized, filled with dread, like watching the beginning of a car crash. Sure enough, he throws the sand, overhead and forward, with enough force that it rains down on each child and woman sitting within three feet of us. Babies cry out as they are stung in the eyes, and older children whip their heads around to see what happened.

The women react quickly, grabbing their kids and moving them away, piercing Nat or me with sharp, angry glances. The whispering begins, the heads bent together, the pointing. My stomach hurts, I get that sick feeling of knowing there's something I should be doing but not knowing what. I understand what these women think of me and my child. Of course I do. I used to be the same way before I knew anything else. Before I knew what it was like to have a different kind of child, or before I knew anything about autism.

Eighteen years later, I see that young, thirty-year-old version of me sitting hunched with shame in the sandbox and I want to stand her up, brush her off, and say, "Oh, come on!" and then buy her a cup of coffee; maybe the other moms too. I imagine myself winking at them, or rolling my eyes, and saying, "Oops, sorry! Everyone OK? Yeah, I hate when he does that!" And then I would find something more appropriate for him to do, or more likely, some eccentric thing Nat enjoyed and that would not bother others, like filling the bucket with water from the water fountain and pouring it out on the pavement, over and over again. Then I would join those other moms on the bench.

As tough as Nat was back then, my own misery about Nat was tougher. Now I realize that grief and misery were not actually imposed on me by Nat, by autism, or by the other women but by my own unresolved feelings and by how I perceived things. To me, autism meant that Nat was no longer the Nat I had known or imagined him to be. I thought I did not know him anymore. Everything he did I now saw through the blurry gray filter of autism. To me, Nat was not throwing the sand the way other kids throw sand. He did not do it out of some child-like impulse to make mischief, to start a fight, or to express himself. No, to me, he was throwing the sand because he was autistic. He was throwing sand because he was the weird one, the disabled one, the different one.

I understood that Nat liked to come to the playground to throw sand and watch the particles shimmer downward in the sunlight—but that seemed like the wrong reason to come to a playground! You were supposed to want to *play* in a play-ground, but he did not play like the other kids, and that was the shameful part.

What ultimately had to change for me to be happier was not other people and was not Nat. It was my way of seeing things. But, at the same time, if the world had sometimes been a little more understanding of Nat and the challenges of raising him, it would have gone a long way toward helping me through it all.

WHEN PEOPLE DON'T UNDERSTAND

It is tough to know what to do when the rest of the world does not show compassion to our children. Many autism parents find that while their child is still in the adorable, little-guy phase, the rest of the world is far more tolerant of aberrant behavior. But as our kids grow up, the public is less and less tolerant of their idiosyncrasies. Amy from Washington says that most people's responses to her son, Nick, were positive when he was still little enough to get away with acting out. Most people were not even aware of his diagnosis. But things have changed for them now that Nick is five. "The first stares happened just recently. For example, we went to our favorite pizza place, and Nick was off running as soon as we got there. My husband was at the counter ordering our food, and I am trying to keep Nick from melting down. During our laps around the dining area, I caught glimpses of people looking at us. It was the Why Can't You Control Your Kid type of look. In my mind, my Momma Bear comes out and screams 'What the hell are you staring at??!'"

Amy continues, "Another time a lady said to me, 'He is too old to be eating baby food.' I answered with, 'He has some texture issues' and just left it at that. [His mouth was so sensitive to contact that it interfered with most of his eating.] But that comment really bugged me. I don't go around telling people what their child should be eating. These people have no idea what we go through every day. They take for granted that their kids will just eat what is put in front of them. We worked for three weeks on getting Nick to eat one piece of cereal—rolling it in his hand, mashing it, touching it to his cheeks, his chin, his lips, and, finally, putting it in his mouth."

For Amy's family, what makes a positive difference in their lives is having neighbors who not only understand but are actually in their corner. "Our neighbors are some of the most lovely people around. They don't judge. They have known Nick now for over a year and marvel at his progress. They notice how he will now come up to them and look into their faces. They don't think twice if we have to go home early because Nick is having a meltdown. They look past all of that and see him as he really is: a wonderful, smart, and sweet little boy."

Penny, a Pennsylvania mom, shares a story of being in public with her daughter, Maddie, during a particularly bad tantrum. "It was a beautiful summer night in Ocean City, New Jersey, on the boardwalk," Penny begins. "We were on our annual summer family vacation. For one week we do what we want when we want. Sounds like a vacation, right? When you have an eleven-year-old daughter with autism, however, it's anything but. 'Going with the flow' is difficult for Maddie, and on this night we reached the breaking point."

Penny continues, "It was nine P.M. The rides had been ridden, and we were ready to head home back down the boardwalk. But my daughter decides that she doesn't want to leave. We do the obligatory ten-minute and five-minute warnings, then we prompt her with 'We are leaving,' and give her the itinerary for the walk home (we will stop here and there; we will get ice cream). Only tonight, my daughter's response is 'I'm going.' In Maddie-speak, this means 'I'm outta here.'"

Maddie started to run, and Penny grabbed her sweatshirt sleeve. "Faster than I can even think, she is down," says Penny, "on her back, on the boardwalk, kicking me as hard as she can and yelling, '*Security! Security! You let me go!!!!*' My husband ushers our other two children to a nearby bench. I start to cry. It hurts to be kicked by an eleven-year-old. I am tired. I am holding on to her wrist and if I let go, all bets are off. I am screwed. I willingly stand there while my eleven-year-old kicks me and yells for help from security. I plead with her to stop kicking and yelling and hurting. It does no good at all. She is lost in the fit, lost to her autism. A crowd soon forms around me. People are staring and saying things under their breath."

Penny's story continues, "A policeman approaches me and his hand is hovering over the billy club on his belt. I think, *What is he gonna do? Hit her? Hit me?* I say through my tears, 'She has autism. Her name is Maddie. She's eleven and having a tantrum. We just need time. I am her mother, you can check my ID in my purse. My name is Penny.' The policeman slowly backs away.

"Twenty minutes later Maddie has calmed down. We are tear-laden, tired, and all of us hurt. The crowd eventually dissipates. We slowly walk on down the boardwalk, and all the while my daughter is sobbing and telling me she is so sorry. I am in tears, too, but they're tears of relief that we survived another one. Walking home, we do indeed get ice cream. Maybe we are celebrating that we got through it. We actually pass by the same policeman who approached us during the episode. What must he think of this eleven-year-old now eating ice cream with her mother? Maybe he got a glimpse into autism and the roller coaster we sometimes feel we are on.

"I don't want pity," Penny says. "I just want understanding that it's damn hard at times. I want compassion—from strangers, from policeman, anyone who might step in and ask

'What can I do to help?' instead of just staring. I want people to assume that I'm doing the best I can, the best anyone can, and that sometimes I am just trying to make it through the event."

Penny adds, "I have a lot of wonderful stories, too, of compassion, of understanding, of just pure love for my daughter and who she is. Honestly, I have plenty more of those than I do of the horrible episodes that have left me broken and defeated. Each time I feel that way, eventually someone does something that leaves me feeling whole and lighter." That, to Penny, is life in its finest form: "It's the yin and the yang of it all. I try not to dwell on the downside. The sun will come up tomorrow and we will still have autism within our family. I can choose how I live it. I do many things in my life that make me happy, with people who love me unconditionally. I guess you would say that makes me content, autism and all."

Penny sees a clear demarcation between those things that have to do with Maddie, those that pertain to the insensitive world, and those that are about herself. But it took me so long to understand that I was my own worst enemy. I cared too much what others thought about Nat's unusual behavior. "No one can make you feel inferior without your permission," is the way Eleanor Roosevelt put it. We can all take a lesson from that.

Joe, a dad from Kentucky, sent me a story of how he and his wife, Anna, coped with an incident of public rudeness toward his eight-year-old autistic son, Jack. "We were on vacation in Orlando and went to SeaWorld. Shortly after we arrived, a thunderstorm rolled in. We were able to take shelter in a place where you could observe the killer whales. It's outside, but there's an overhang. Jack hates thunder. He screamed for about thirty to forty-five minutes, including ordering the rain to stop. There were probably about twenty or thirty other people waiting out the storm there. Most people kept to themselves and a few were supportive. I'm sure they all wanted Jack to stop (I know I did). At a certain point two boys actually 'shushed' Jack. I said something about how Jack was doing his best. My wife later told me she heard the parents talking to these two boys about how Jack was a bad boy and we weren't good parents. My wife then told them Jack was possessed by the devil, shrugged her shoulders, and walked to the other side of the observation area where Jack and I were!"

Unfortunately, it's a common experience for most autism parents, at one time or another, to feel humiliated by strangers. Or, if it is not humiliation, then we might experience just plain lack of understanding. Paulette, who calls herself my twin sister in Alabama, told me of the challenges she faces going into public with her daughter Punkin. "Punkin and I have had some good experiences and some bad experiences. I really understand other autism parents when they say how proud they are just to be able to go places and it's normal. I am invited to go and see *The Nutcracker* ballet for Christmas. I have decided that Punkin will not be going. Everyone wants to know why I am not taking her when my best friend is taking her girls. I find myself getting defensive." Paulette has a long memory of her experiences out in the world with Punkin, and it makes her think twice about going anywhere with her, just like I still do with Nat. "This summer," she said, "when it was just the two of us and the meltdowns were happening on a regular basis, I couldn't get anybody to help me—but they are still quick to criticize my decision not to take her to the ballet."

Paulette continues, "They just don't know how much I would love to take her, but this is going to be a trip that I take just for me. Most of the time when we go places, I say, 'This is for Punkin,' and if I have to spend a little time in the restroom calming her down, it's OK because I am doing it for her. But when we get up because she needs to go somewhere else to calm down, nobody gets up and says, 'Do you need any help?' Yet they still want to criticize."

It can be especially difficult to navigate the social pressures around Christmas and other holiday times. At these times of year, I've had to think hard about how to create peace of mind for myself. I've also had to find ways of articulating and affirming our needs to others, especially if we are going into a social situation where the adults involved just don't understand autism.

Going to Places and Events Where They Just Don't Get Autism

- Ask yourself where *you* want to be. Is it possible to be *there*, instead of at the unwelcoming place? Find out.

- Don't be afraid to leave children at home for an evening or a special event, the way Paulette decided to leave Punkin so that she could enjoy the ballet without worries.

- If it's not possible to get out of the obligation or to leave your child at home, is it possible to shorten your time at this event? Discuss solutions with your partner or hosts. (You could strike bargains, for example, with your husband: "If we come home early, I won't bother you while you watch the game." Or, with the host: "If we can have the dinner at your house this year, I'll do it next year." Having control over these events can help you to relax.)

- If you must attend a gathering you don't enjoy, come up with one escape for yourself: figure out how you can get away from there for an hour on a walk, for example. Physical exercise is the best way to clear your head and make your body feel good. If that's not possible, can you even run an errand with that person, so that you have time in the car to vent? Or call a friend on your cell phone! You need getaway time.

- What are you eating? Food makes a big difference in how you feel. Bring your favorite treats with you in addition to your hostess gift—a favorite wine, chocolate, cheese, whatever it is you really look forward to, and choose your moment to eat it.

- When you come back home, or when all of your guests leave, take it easy by ordering takeout or going out to dinner if you can. Just be sure dinner is easy, whatever it is. We sometimes have "breakfast for dinner," which for us is pancakes from a mix and eggs.

FINDING LIFELINES

Probably the most helpful happiness strategy for an autism parent is finding lifelines. Lifelines are the people in our lives, outside of our spouses or partners, who truly understand our children. Lifelines are the people who "get it," as many autism parents say. You can leave your kid with a lifeline for a period of time—an hour, a weekend, it can vary—and you don't have to worry about it. These are the folks who let us escape and rejuvenate. Lifelines help our children, too, because they provide them with bonding experiences beyond Mom and Dad and help them to develop more independence.

For many of us, lifelines are our own extended families. In my case, both sets of grandparents have always been helpful and accepting. My children have stayed with my parents on many overnights, and on those occasions they have drawn closer to their grandparents, and they have learned things from them, such as new kinds of chores (for example, washing my dad's car or cleaning up fallen twigs from the yard).

My father presents the kids with a demeanor that's part demanding grandpa, part cheerleader. This attitude helps especially with Nat, who seems to enjoy all of the attention he gets at my parents' house.

Dad finds the positive, or at least the humorous, in just about everything that happens in his life, and Nat is no exception. My entire family is like that: Mom always tries to read with Nat and to keep up with his hobbies, bringing him gifts and treats that match his interests. And my sister, Laura, takes Nat on walks, regularly, because they both have so much energy that they need to get outside!

With his positive attitude, my father was able to teach Nat how to ride a bike. "With the bike, I kind of did with Nat what I did with you," Dad told me proudly when he explained how he accomplished this. "I stood behind him and held the seat. He already knew how to pedal. Once he got his balance, I ran behind him." My father is extremely proud of being the one to teach Nat such a complicated thing as bicycling, and they ride together even now, on Cape Cod vacations. This gives Nat and Dad joy—and it gives me a break.

Paulette, too, has a lifeline in her sisters. "I'm single," she says, "and I don't have any friend who can really say, 'I understand.' But one of her sisters takes care of Punkin for a couple of days a week. Paulette's other sister has a kid with Williams syndrome—a rare neurological disorder—so they really identify with each other.

Dyanne, a friend from Massachusetts, has a teenage son with Asperger's, and she says she has learned a lot about how to get what she needs from other adults and how to avoid what she doesn't need. "Find those people who don't freeze up around your kid, who deal well with his eccentricities. Surround yourself with them," she says. For Dyanne, certain friends of hers have been the saving grace. Her longtime friend Joan, a veteran kindergarten teacher, was the one who first noticed that as a toddler Patrick seemed to lack spatial awareness. She urged Dyanne to get him evaluated, and Dyanne knew she could trust Joan's instincts.

Another friend, Lee, has often helped Dyanne function and stay positive. "Lee has worked with special-needs kids for years," she told me. Lee's can-do attitude helped Dyanne, as did Lee's way of seeing Patrick and Dyanne as just a mom and a kid with particular difficulties that could be resolved with some planning. For example, when Patrick was little, Dyanne wanted to attend a christening. Lee helped her to strategize: "Bring toys! They're not going to care. It's only *you* who might feel funny." Dyanne admitted to me that back then she never would have imagined bringing toys, snacks, and books to a christening, but Lee helped her to realize that she could decide for herself what was right for her family.

Larger communities and organizations have often been welcoming to Dyanne and Patrick, but not always. "We did Little League when Pat was four. The coaches were incredible." What made the coaches get it? "They were all dads," Dyanne answered. Boosted by the Little League experience, they tried soccer; but this was a whole different thing. "Parents were yelling, and the coaches were younger kids. Pat didn't understand what he was supposed to do, and they were so stuck on the rules."

Luckily, Dyanne was not discouraged by this negative experience with soccer. She tried Special Olympics and found that it was exactly what they were looking for. "It was a whole different world," Dyanne said reverently. I knew exactly what she meant, for there we were, sitting side by side at the basketball court while Pat and Nat ran around and shot baskets with their teammates of three years. We weren't even watching them; we felt comfortable enough to just sit at the sidelines and talk to each other, completely confident that Pat and Nat would be just fine.

Like Dyanne, I have had to go by trial and error to find successful venues for Nat's social experiences. Because of the prevalence of Special Olympics, autism parents often first make their forays into the outside world through sports. But it is important to figure out which kind of sport is right for your child. We found, at first, that Nat did not do as well with team sports such as T-ball because he could not attend to all of the interactions that went on between his teammates. At the time, that concept was beyond his abilities: he did not know to watch the hitter in order to decide to run to the next base; and he did not know that he had to catch the ball and try to tag an opposing teammate.

We might have stopped there, discouraged, but we kept our minds open and found a sport that was more individualized: gymnastics offered through the Special Olympics. The college-age coach knew nothing about autism, yet ended up with a gold-medal team because the parents educated her—and she was willing to learn. The first day, there were a lot of gangly autistic boys literally bouncing off the gym walls (because there was a large trampoline in there). All was chaos. Some of us shook our heads and started to feel that old familiar feeling of discouragement. But we did not give up. This young woman was so sunny and kind; we knew she had potential. So we sat her down and told her to use simple, repetitious instructions and to follow the same routine for each class. This way the kids knew what to expect and could follow through when it came time for the meets.

It feels like a blessing when a special person outside of my immediate family connects with Nat, the way Jocelyn, his gymnastics coach, did. Jocelyn was always willing to work with Nat, even when he was going through a very aggressive phase. She presented him with the same wide smile and lightheartedness each session, and he never was aggressive to her. She even came to our home and took him to the playground for some extra gymnastic sessions, during a very unstable time for the family. Like my father teaching Nat how to ride a bike, Jocelyn got the best out of him because she expected the most from him; she took it for granted that he would rise to it. She saw only the potential in him. I understand the difficulties involved in trying to connect with Nat: wondering whether he wants to interact at that moment, worrying about upsetting him somehow, not wanting to be rejected by him. We are all human and none of us wants to fail at anything we've attempted. So I have come to believe that those who do try with Nat, and especially those who succeed, are giving us a real gift.

All autism parents need more people like that in our lives, and we must keep on looking for them, and try to move on quickly if a given situation is not working out. Many of our experiences with our children out in the world are mixed, so when one thing doesn't work out, it is helpful if we don't scrap the entire effort, but rather look for a slightly different path to the same goal, the way gymnastics rather than T-ball worked for Nat.

Of course if we can learn to recognize the truly empathic people in our midst, even if the encounter is brief, we become stronger and more capable for future experiences out in the world. My friend Cathy from Connecticut told me about a "watershed event" in her family's life, a small but meaningful moment when she learned that sometimes strangers can be kind and downright helpful with our autistic kids. "Last fall we took the kids to a 'family fun' event at an apple orchard. A local newspaper photographer descended on us (we were like sitting ducks on our picnic blanket). He tried to get Jack to cooperate with getting his photo taken, and I said something like 'Um, he has developmental issues,' something I would have preferred to avoid saying.

"The photographer asked, 'Is he a little autistic?' When I replied that yes, Jack was autistic, I expected the photographer to give up instantly. Instead he grew more intent on getting Jack's photo. And guess whose photo ended up on the front page in that week's paper!"

Fielding, a father from Tennessee, wrote to me about one particular victory he experienced with his autistic daughter in public. His way of telling the story reflects his wonderful attitude. "My daughter has been doing a lot better and I told her that if she did good at ABA, I would buy her a movie. We went to Wal-Mart, picked out the movie, walked through the toy department without her stopping or melting down on the way to the checkout, and then she waited nicely in a long line. I was on Cloud Nine! You would think my kid had just graduated from Harvard! She did say 'Let's go!' a couple of times while we waited for the clerk to fold one of the nine shirts a guy farther up the line was purchasing, or while we waited for a lady to get her thirty assorted snack foods checked out, but all in all it was a *great* experience."

Fielding continues. "The next week, I thought I would see if it was a fluke, so we repeated the whole thing. I purposefully picked the longest checkout line. This time, you would think she had won the Nobel Prize. I was one proud autism dad!"

How to Stay Sane and Smiling in an Often Insensitive World

- Reassure yourself that you are not the only one who has a square-peg child in a round-hole world. Take a look at the book *Shut Up about . . . Your Perfect Kid!* at shutupabout.com.

- Come up with a set response or rejoinder to ward off offensive comments without getting into a huge entanglement. Here's one I like: "My son is autistic. What's *your* excuse?" Confident humor can work, though simplicity is probably the best course. For example, "I'm doing the best I can, and so is he." As much as possible, take the high road. As Ned often tells me, "It's best to assume that people are ignorant more often than they are malicious." At the same time, remember that you don't owe anybody any explanations. They're the ones with the bad manners, after all!

- Hang on to hope: just because an activity is not working out today, it doesn't mean that it never will work out. Think of Dyanne, who had Patrick try many different sports before he found the best fit.

- Look for your lifelines, or cultivate some if you don't have any. Support groups or church groups might be resources for you.

- Set yourself up for success by going out there with support. Try activities with organizations that already get it, such as Special Olympics and autism support-group outings. Find the groups with the most support so that you can get a break, hanging out on the sidelines with other parents or even just reading a book for a little while.

- For a true high, participate in one of the "autism walks" that happen all over the country, and in other countries now as well. You will find yourself among thousands who are dealing with the exact same things as you and your family. Go to AutismSpeaks.org to find out about the "autism walk" nearest to you.

7

Letting Go

When Our Kids Leave Home

AT THE AGE OF EIGHTEEN, Nat moved out of our home to live at his school, and the void that opened up in my life nearly swallowed me whole. In some ways, it felt like his early childhood days all over again. It was a cruel twist on those days, however, because back then I was full of him, trying to make room for this utterly new, fresh life, the most important thing that had ever happened to me. So when he left home, my heart, which had stretched so far for him, felt gaping and torn.

I went through weeks of crying, just like during the diagnosis days. But this time there was a difference: I knew now how to take care of myself: by writing, dancing, and especially by pounding out my pain through hard exercise. I went on long, hard bike rides, or ran at the reservoir in the hot August sun. I danced until I developed plantar fasciitis (terrible heel pain), but I kept right on dancing, because my emotional pain was far worse. I also wrote poems and blog posts. I went to a therapist. I cried a lot to Ned and to my parents.

During moments of clarity and respite from my grief, I realized that I would now have a lot more time for myself; time that was unfettered by the daily worry of how Nat would fit into my—and the other boys'—schedule. When Nat lived here, I always had to think about four o'clock, when the van dropped him off from school, and what the other two boys would need to do, and how Nat would be with that. With Nat gone from my day, a lot of psychological energy became available.

At some point, it occurred to me that exercise and writing alone were not enough for me anymore. I decided to get a job outside of the home, for the first time in twenty years. I wanted to try to teach English at a nearby college. With my writing experience, it seemed like a good fit. I set about the process of job hunting and quickly landed a part-time teaching job at Suffolk University.

I loved the job immediately; I was really ready to be out of the house, commuting on the train, out in the world among people. I think it also helped that my students were Nat's age. It felt healing somehow to look out at those sweet young faces—even the irritating, overly rambunctious students—and teach them how to write better, and maybe even how to love it. I guess I even acted somewhat maternal with them, and they seemed to welcome it. It turned out to be a nicely symbiotic relationship that was very comforting to me.

Along with all the preparation necessary for my new job—lesson plans, reading, organizing myself—I spent a lot of time gathering the rest of my family around me in new configurations. It was the four of us now, without Nat, and this was almost dizzying in its potential. We went out to dinner on the spur of the moment. We went out to movies without worrying about sudden tantrums. Ned and I went out as much as when we had first begun dating, confidently leaving Ben (now ten) at home with Max (now sixteen). Even with the new job and my writing projects, our lives had become so simple. I felt I had a glimpse of what my family could have been like without battling the hardships that come with autism. And then I would feel the searing pain of guilt. How dare I enjoy myself because Nat had moved out? How could I be making plans with our newfound freedom and free time—without Nat around? It seemed heartless sometimes. But there it was.

How did this huge change in our lives begin? It may have started with a moment like the following, from my blog, or perhaps it culminated from many such moments: "The back of my hands are bloody and my spirits are low. Big struggle this morning with Nat. He would not sit down in time-out this time. That's a first. His arm is a mess from his biting. He let me clean and bandage it. I was struck by the odd juxtaposition of a little blue bunny-shaped ice pack sitting atop Nat's muscular, bloody and bruised forearm."

I had written this post during the winter that Nat was eighteen. I still can't get the image out of my head of Ben racing upstairs to escape as Nat came close to him. "Dad! He's biting his arm again!" he had shouted in panic. Nat's arm biting often precedes lashing out at others.

That morning I got dressed without showering and ran downstairs to help. I tried desperately to smile so that Ben would focus on school and not his fear of Nat's imminent aggression. Ned hurried Ben off to school while I stayed with Nat, not wanting to leave him and Max alone. Although in the end nothing worse happened, I remember a familiar, old feeling, as if I was guarding Max, even though Max is so big.

After that incident, I set up a meeting with our team to talk about planning Nat's residential placement. In the early fall of that year Ned and I had gone on a tour of some group homes run by Nat's school, and we had gotten an idea of what they could offer. We were told there was a waiting list, which was a good thing, because it gave us time to plan and make the transition—all of us.

I told myself that Nat was eighteen and that it was not horrible of me to plan this. I also told myself that such a move probably was better for Nat, who would have round-the-clock structure, and that it would be better for Ben not to have to live with fear. Ned told me this, too, though it took a few months for him to really feel that it was the truth. Later on he confessed that part of him felt we should have been able to handle Nat ourselves, but that at the same time he felt a kind of relief not to have to. He said that because the pieces were falling into place (our school system supported the move), he was able to shift into feeling positive about our decision.

None of Ned's certainty prepared me for the terrible sadness of watching Nat move out. The last day of our summer vacation on Cape Cod signaled the end of Nat's living with us full time; he was to move out in early August. I wrote the following poem from the deck of our vacation house, to express and ease some of my pain:

Last Day

Healed by love and sleep
Awakened to your voice that told you things.
I marvel at how you comfort yourself
I wonder if you sat down with me for more
I know you don't want to leave this place of softest
*   blues and spiky greens,*
Crows that argue and rabbits that chew, stare, and
*   think—maybe.*
This goodbye feels like more to me
A familiar maw of sadness yawns open as the day
*   closed.*
We're going.
You're going.
I drink scalding coffee, swallow down fresh blooming
*   pain*
and listen to you whispering sudden cool laughter
*   bubbles in your mouth*
And a symphony of birds outside
On our last day.

It was not that Nat *wasn't* ready to go. It was that I was not ready for him to go. We went from zero to sixty, or actually, sixty to zero, just like that: from having Nat under our roof, an integral part of our family life, shaping us with his intensity, his special needs, and his unique spirit, for eighteen years. Then, suddenly, in one day, we packed him up, and just like that, he was living someplace else. We felt stunned, a little directionless at first. Yes, our last summer together was hard, so hard, with frequent outbursts. But for him to no longer be there, and all of the difficulties suddenly lifted—this felt wrong to me, too light, too simple.

However lost I felt, there was no doubt that this move had to happen. Ben was so afraid of Nat, no matter what I did. If I said too much to explain things to him, it would only serve to invalidate his feelings. I didn't know how much of what I'd said to Ben had sunk in. All I knew was how he had grown to hate Nat (or so he believed), and to hate just about everything in his life, to mistrust us, to withdraw into sarcasm, Goth clothing, gaming, cynicism, tears. In our family frieze, Ben's troubles stood out in high relief. Ben was in great need of help. I had to focus on Ben as much as on Nat, a nightmarish, *Sophie's Choice* kind of dilemma. Ben seemed to be crying out for help, struggling in school, struggling with friends, angry at home, easily brought to tears.

I never blamed Nat; I would never see it that way. Well, I tried not to blame him. Sometimes, it did feel like Nat could have controlled himself and just did not. I'm sure it felt that way to Ben most of the time. But for the most part, I'm pretty clear that I don't blame autism for the difficulties in our life. Autism itself is a condition of nerve cells, like a part of Nat's body; to blame him for it would be pointless, like blaming my own belly for having cellulite, or blaming the humidity for causing the rain.

But that summer I did, on some level, come to terms with the fact that it was indeed time for Nat to go. There were so many indicators pointing in that direction. He was old enough and could likely learn more about how to be with others by living in the group home, where he would also have one-on-one training from an aide. Nat would probably be all right, I had to admit. Nat's school was a place I could trust, which was saying a lot; I don't trust easily. It has taken me years to get to know his school and how they do things. I know their flaws and I know their positive attributes. Teacher after teacher seems to fall in love with him, and why wouldn't they? He's bright and beautiful, laughs easily, and he's so funny.

We quickly got to know Donnie Kimbrel, the program co-ordinator at the residential program where Nat was living. Donnie has been working with complicated kids (behavioral issues, aggression problems) since 1995. He started as direct-care staff with agencies such as the Department of Youth Services and the Department of Social Services in Massachusetts.

I first met Donnie when I was driving around what would be Nat's new neighborhood. I had not made an appointment; I just wanted to check out the environment, slipping in under the radar. A young man was setting out trash barrels in front of the house. Knowing how careful the school is about the kids' privacy, and how the public interacts with them, I did not think that a surprise visit would be a good thing. Also, I didn't want to seem like a snoop or an overly controlling mother (which I suppose I am). But I wanted to see what it felt like there, without any official from the school shaping my perceptions.

Donnie saw me, so I approached him tentatively and asked, "Is this a—uh—school residence?"

Donnie looked at me for a second, then broke into a grin and with sparkling eyes said, "You must be Nat's mom!" and we shook hands. It felt like we understood each other right away. What a relief to know that the person running the house was this warm and good-humored young man!

Donnie nearly always has that same wry smile on his face, and an intelligence and warmth come through in the way he deals with people—from demanding parents to their demanding children—that seem to say that he's seen it all, but that he enjoys what he's seen. Donnie told me about the many positive experiences he's had throughout his career, even though they have been very difficult at times. After talking to him over the months, I realized that his viewpoint about his students and autism made me feel happier and more optimistic, about Nat and about life in general. I think it is crucial for autism parents to surround themselves with people who make us feel that way: that everything is all right, and that many things are possible. Donnie has had the experiences to back that up, too.

One late afternoon during the summer of Nat's move, I was dozing off, tired from a hard run and wanting to shut down my mind a little. I was feeling a big, oppressive ache about Nat that just would not go away. (A heart migraine was what I was calling it.)

As my eyes closed, this thought came to me: *You don't have to do it. You can keep him home with you.* I remembered then how I had had similar thoughts way back when he was three and everyone was telling me he needed to go to school. I wanted to keep him home, to keep him away from this cruel, demanding world. I would teach him everything myself. I didn't want to deal with special education laws, bureaucracies, methodologies, professionals. I didn't want to deal with my fears and sadness. I especially did not want to deal with his difficulties with the world.

Ned, ever the cool washcloth on my feverish brow (or the splash of cold water in my face), had said to me back then, "You can't do that. You would never be able to be his teacher. It's a huge job and you're tired as it is." Something like that. Yet those rebellious thoughts came back to me sometimes, and I felt a secret power from knowing that if I didn't like it, he would not have to go. Just like that. And if he didn't like it, he could just come home. I didn't care what anyone said or thought. *I am Mommy, hear me roar.* This thinking helped me for a little while. Sometimes a little bit of denial, of living in a little fantasy world (without taking any action), helps me get through some terrible times, such as saying goodbye to Nat that summer.

But all in all, I was in rough shape. At the end of July, as we approached the move-out date, I decided it would help me (and perhaps Nat, and all of the family) if we threw Nat a going-away party, like we would have done if he were going off to college. It would provide not only a fun distraction, it could also help transform this difficult passage into a cause to celebrate.

As these things go with me, the idea quickly germinated and I flew into action, inviting family before Ned was completely on board. This is our usual pattern, however, and Ned was soon into the planning as much as I was. I designed a cake that was to be a three-dimensional model of Nat's new home, a gray clapboard residence, with the kids all standing outside, and Donnie right behind them. I handed over the drawing to a local bakery that I knew would be up to the task. I rented a moonbounce and worked it out with Donnie that the entire residence would be there, along with the necessary staff. I also invited friends from Nat's old school, and all of his Special Olympics teammates.

On the afternoon of the party, Donnie showed up with two vans filled with guys and our yard was transformed into a gigantic carnival, with wild moonbounce jumping, autistic kids flapping their arms and whooping joyously, while parents and staff stood by smiling and chatting. And the cake was perfect.

I think that the party really helped Nat—and all of us—grasp the concept that moving out was a reason to be happy. (Cake always helps convey happy messages.) Even though it might have been confusing to him to see all those staffers and students in our yard, out of context, I have to believe that it was at the same time comforting for him to see that his different homes could connect together easily. I know it was for me.

In August, just after Nat moved out, I would try to remember the good feelings I felt at the party, and try to think about

Donnie and all the good things Nat was moving toward. But then I would pass his room. Looking around at all the toys, from the past eighteen years of his life, the class photos, the art, just sucked my spirit downward. I saw the aborted attempts to teach him this and that: sentence-generation puzzles, construction toys, a piggy bank, a baby doll, math flash cards. I saw the toys he used to like, now just dust magnets: Funny Bunny (tattered gray rags shaped vaguely like a rabbit), books on tape, Disney CDs.

I still have to remind myself at times that he is moving forward, progressing, perhaps to something better. He is going to learn so much from Donnie and the well-trained staff there, make friends with the guys in his house, and do so many more activities than he can here. And I have to give myself all the time I need to get used to his being gone and find ways to make myself happy.

I am able to find comfort and inspiration in thinking about what Donnie has shared with me about his work. "More than anything," said Donnie, "dealing with autistic students is what you make of it," he said. "You always have to try to find a different way to make something happen . . . you have to learn to adapt." He explained that just plain listening is the way he has forged relationships with challenging children: "You listen to a person to really know that person's ins and outs. With autism, it's just a different form of listening. A student might not be able to tell you if he's in pain, but he might give you a visual clue," like rocking suddenly, or excessive hand-flapping.

Donnie has learned that the attitude that is most helpful

to his work is one of empathy and connection. Tuning in this way, Donnie is able to make things happen for his guys, where others might be reluctant to even try. "This is not a glamorous job," Donnie told me. "How many people wake up in the morning and say, 'I can't wait to go in and clean poop, I can't wait to go in and get bitten.' But the rewards you get—for example, when we went out to Worcester and came home with the gold medals from the Special Olympics basketball team I had coached, I was so proud of those guys that everything negative that had ever happened to me in my career just went out the window after that."

Even knowing how well cared for Nat is, I find that I rarely simply move forward. I seem to go back in time a lot, looking for emotional scabs to pick, or new therapies or approaches, thinking I am escaping pain when usually I am only delaying it. But maybe that's not so bad, as long as I can catch myself at it—or if Ned can.

Unlike me, NancyBea was certain, right at the start, that the decision to move Henry into the residences at his school was the right thing to do. "It's been great in many ways," she says. "*He* is so much happier there. That was really clear from day one. We just were not able to provide what he needed. This was hard to accept, but not too hard. When he was home, we just felt that he wasn't happy, and that we weren't helping him grow in any meaningful way. He wasn't learning any academics, he wasn't learning any self-help skills. We were just trying to survive, trying to get through the day, and that wasn't good for anybody."

When I asked her how it's been for Henry at the new residence, she said, "The whole setup there is good for him. There are constant activities and constant schedules. The downside is that when he comes home, he's extra bored. And when he's with us, I'm not able to devote all my time to just taking care of him. I guess that's selfish," she said, a little defensively. But I told her that I didn't think it was, that I completely understood and felt some of the same things about myself—with a lot of guilt, of course.

She continued, "I think that we always thought that at some point we weren't going to be able to handle him." When they found out about a school from a friend, they visited it to evaluate its potential for Henry. There they saw a kid who to them seemed just like Henry. This child made them think that Henry could actually learn and be happy there.

Then they had to deal with the special education administrators in her school system, who wanted them to try the public school program instead. But NancyBea visited the proposed placement, and knew it was wrong for Henry. "When I saw that program, I could tell that it was just going to be more babysitting. So we went ahead and placed him in the private school without the school district agreeing to it." A terrible legal fight ensued, but NancyBea held to her decision by reminding herself that Henry's future was at stake, and that up until then no one had been able to help him. The private school felt so right to her, and she was determined to make it happen. "I had to get up and present my case to really hostile school officials, who were trying to tell me that the placement wasn't appropriate, and I had to say, 'Oh yes it is!'"

The school district eventually agreed to the private placement. But to get there, NancyBea had to go to the angry, action-oriented side of herself—to get in touch with her own power. Grieving and being sad is not everybody's way, and it is important to figure out which emotions are helpful to you and your child and at what time. Anger has helped me keep my resolve at many a team meeting.

Coming to Terms with Residential Placement

- Let yourself mourn. Cry, sleep, complain. Feel angry if you need to, but try to channel it into positive action, like NancyBea did.

- Write about how you feel or what you're going through when you can't talk about it.

- For some, prayers or affirmations help them get through a difficult passage like this one. Autism mom Suzanne likes the following Web site, which sends you affirmations: affirmationplanet.com; or this one, specifically for autism families: childrenofdestiny.org. Zoe from Maryland prays daily, thanking God for her family and life. She also feels calmed by reading a philosopher called

Krishnamurti. I also pray; I find the Jewish "Shehecheyanu" to be a wonderful, all-purpose prayer of affirmation: http://en.wikipedia.org/wiki/Shehecheyanu.

- Remember to get exercise. Getting those endorphins going lifts the spirits.

- I get a great deal of reassurance from the National Family Caregivers Association Web site (thefamilycaregiver.org). It is important and comforting to hear from professional caregivers of the disabled about the dedication, commitment, and passion they have toward their work.

- Although a good cry can relieve some of the pressure on our hearts, we have to know when to stop crying and find a simple pursuit that can help us reconnect with our lives. Check out the following wonderful Web site to learn ways to simplify your life and to get some perspective on what's truly important: zenhabits.net.

- Stay connected to your partner. Staying connected might just be about letting both of you handle grief in your own way (through Internet research, heavy exercise, eating chocolate). Maybe having small conversations about your feelings, just letting the other express them without any recrimination. Sometimes in the worst moments comes the best clarity. If you do not have a marital partner, maintain a connection with the person in your life who most understands you and what you're going through, whether it's a sibling, your parents, your neighbor, or an Internet autism buddy.

- If you can, mark the passage beforehand with something positive, such as a party, a special outing, or a present for your child.

- Know that your grief will pass. Trust me, it always does.

When Nat came home on his first visit from school, I wrote in my blog, "Natty is home. I am not going to be able to get enough hugging and kissing in because, just like his brothers, this guy needs his space! But I am used to adoring from a distance, and I will just let my eyes drink him in."

Almost immediately after he arrived, he went upstairs, where I found him curled up on my bed. Sometimes he likes to nap there. I lay down next to him, facing his back, and asked him about his new house. His voice was small and muffled; he just wanted to sleep.

I felt transported back, way back, to when Nat was a baby. I remembered lying down in my bed with him next to me, hoping we could just nap there. I was so tired! But little Nat thought I was playing a game. Every few seconds he would raise his sweet head and look at me and laugh.

The memory of little Nat and the sleep game danced before my eyes, almost as real as the sleeping, grown-up Nat in front of me. Now that he was back, just for that one night,

I was sharply aware that those babyhood days were over. He was now living in a different home, and that was the way it was supposed to be. And it was so good to have him here, to have all my guys home with me. Three strapping young men, with their lives stretching out ahead of them, and the hot blue sky overhead the only limit.

In talking to my parents network, I was not surprised to find how many of our most painful experiences are about separation from our children. These are often as acute as the pain of first finding out the diagnosis. As difficult as it has been to raise our special-needs children, to live with all that struggle, the beginnings of letting go are excruciating in a different way. And yet, there are also distinct joys and benefits to that process.

Dyanne, my friend from Massachusetts told me how hard it was for her when Patrick, who has Asperger's, was about to enter his freshman year of high school. His transition to high school was a big milestone for him, because he had been at the same elementary school with many of the same kids for so many years; everyone knew him there. Dyanne worried a lot about how much he would need to understand to navigate the social complexities there. One of the first things she decided she needed to do was to clue Patrick in on what his typically developing peers thought about some very important topics. The first thing she did was to tell him that there was no Santa Claus. She explained to me that she did this because she was afraid he could be targeted by other kids if they knew that he was so naive.

What Dyanne was not prepared for was her son's self-confidence and crystal-clear view of the world. After she finished telling him that Santa didn't actually exist, she waited nervously for his response. Had she crushed him? Would he be angry, tearful? But Patrick considered what she had said for a moment and then replied in his low, serious, adult voice, completely straight-faced, "Can I choose not to believe you?"

Perspective is a gift of getting older. My father often reminds me that he struggled with certain issues when he was my age, and how getting older grants you the ability to see beyond them, and to let go, even with a smile. It is true. My therapist once asked me to picture that younger me, struggling with something or other, and what I would say to her now, if I could. I felt so much compassion for that more innocent self. I felt like my own mother.

It took about six months after Nat moved out for me to adjust and to not be sad all the time. My grief was becoming more and more manageable. I think that's because I was able to stay connected to him. So much of my relationship with Nat exists unseen, in the air between us, in the realm of quiet feeling and of just being next to each other. In those first few months I was lost without that, so I allowed myself to see him or talk to him whenever I felt like it. I kept calling and visiting. I took him out for picnics, for breakfasts, and for ice cream. I would burst into his new home, to his classroom, often with very little warning. The staff and the teachers put up with it. They understood what I was going through (but they did ask me to try to let them know more in advance).

Thus I kept up my bond with Nat, as intensely as ever, while slowly letting go where I had to.

A formative moment in my own progress happened during an autumn afternoon, around two months after the move-out, when I spontaneously took Nat out for lunch at a fancy restaurant. I had, at first, thought nothing of this outing, because for years we have been able to take Nat out to eat. But we had never taken him to a place as nice as this one, and—more important—I had never taken him out to a fancy restaurant *alone*.

As we ate, I remember feeling keenly aware of how nice it was, eating in this pretty, elegant place with my grown-up child. I thought then about how I had never done this before, but that also, today, I had not even considered *not* doing it.

I kept glancing at Nat, so composed, such a delightful young man, and so well behaved that, I realized, no one around us would ever guess he had a profound disability. To think that this was the same person who had sometimes made me feel imprisoned by his unpredictable behavior. Who, at age two, had cried incessantly at every family gathering. Who, when he was four, cried and yelled through an entire meal at a Cape Cod restaurant while the host tried to get either him to stop or us to leave. Who, at eight, had tossed a piece of chicken or something into the air and it hit a man at a nearby table. I could go on and on about all the difficult and unpredictable phases Nat has been through.

Back then, I would never have believed that, several years later, this, too, would be Nat.

I kept imagining an observer at another table, listening to our staccato, syncopated, but acceptable conversation. The way Nat would look at me, dutifully, politely, when I spoke to him, and how he would answer me, though clearly he would rather have been eating his delicious chicken parmesan.

I was listening in on the people at the tables around us: the annoying women behind us who were so squeaky and loud; the men eating together, one of whom kept looking over at us from time to time. Nat and I ate quietly, just a mom and her son, and as I looked at him in our silence, I felt my pride rise up and cover me like a warm, heavy blanket.

After my wonderful little lunch, I realized that I was now living my future, the thought of which, years ago, had many times made me feel so depressed and fearful. All that I had wondered about—Nat's living in a home rather than on his own, Nat's not being able to talk much, Nat's having a low-level job in some back room of a restaurant, his eccentric behavior in public, and most of all my relationship with him—all of that was now right there in front of me. And nothing was as horrible as what I had imagined. Yet it was still exactly what I had imagined.

Similarly, when I used to think about what a group home was like, the images would fill me with despair: spacey adults lolling around a television, being packed into vans for sad little outings to the mall, no one talking to each other. Yet sometimes that is what I see at Nat's new home, but now I don't feel like there's anything wrong with this, because there is actually so much more to it than what it looks like. Yes, the others in the house seem spacey and not talkative, but if you start a conversation with one or another of Nat's house-mates, you will get a response, sometimes helped along by the staff. And when you walk into the living room there, the young men do notice you and their eyes flicker with recognition and interest. And yes, they do get into the vans and go to the mall sometimes, but it is not a mindless pursuit; it is to practice their purchasing and out-in-the-community skills, which is just a way of saying that they need regular exposure to how to act toward others out in public, and the public needs the experience of interacting with them, too.

Nat, in fact, does have a job in the back room of a restaurant, putting together pizza boxes at Papa Gino's Pizzeria, and he loves it. He is an excellent worker, according to his job coaches and his employers, so much so that they are beginning to phase out the job coaches—after only a few months of his working there. His employers are thrilled with him. Everyone who deals with him these days—from supervisors to teachers—is impressed with his independence and his great attitude.

STAYING CONNECTED

When Nat calls home these days, our phone conversations are very different from any other interaction we shared before his move-out. He never says, "No talk to Mommy." He gets right on the phone, and even though his voice trembles with some unnamed emotion, he always talks to me now and answers my questions. He provides content, which is a very new development. He will tell me which chores he did on a given day, which friend he played a game with, or what kind of exercise he chose, for example. Because the answers vary from day to day, I know that he is thinking about his answers and being accurate—as opposed to when he was living at home, when he would have mostly "default" answers. For example, when he was living at home, if I asked him, "What did you do at school, Nat?" he'd say, "Played in school," and that would be the end of it.

Rote responses are still a problem at times, but now I know to reframe the question. If he tells me that he had "noodles and chicken" for dinner three days in a row, I suspect that he is answering this way without thought, because it is easier for him to access those words. So I say, "What *else* did you have for dinner, Nat?" And then I get better information.

It is as if, by leaving home, Nat has been propelled to another level where perhaps he now feels the need to communicate with me in a way I will understand. I believe that he needs, more than ever, to connect and he seems to be aware of that.

I, too, feel that need, and this has led me to try to find other ways to understand what is going on with him. A few weeks after he moved out, on one of his visits home, I found myself feeling a great hunger to talk with him and make up for lost time, but our attempts at direct conversation were labored and flat. I remember sitting on the living room couch watching with such longing while he did his customary circuit from living room to hallway to dining room, waving his arms, stomping, and talking to himself in his unique language. He has nearly always used self-talk, even as a little boy (I used to call it "silly talk" until I realized that this seemed like a put-down), and there have been times when he would insert a familiar word here and there, but I could rarely attribute it to anything going on around him.

As I sat there this time, however, listening to the lilting patterns in his odd phrases, I realized I could recognize the word at the end of each phrase, and that those final words made a kind of sense to me. When he would first come into the house, for example, he'd run upstairs and unpack his bag, which is a very important home routine to him. Eventually I noticed that, as he did this, his self-talk was sprinkled heavily with one intelligible word: *bag*.

After that, I listened more carefully and heard lots of recognizable words—words such as *Mommy, cookies, Max* (when he got home), *bag* (when he wanted me to zip closed my handbag; he hates seeing an open handbag). Sometimes I would break in on his monologue, saying, "What about Max, Nat?" And he would say, "No Max. Mommy will go back to computer," because I had my laptop with me at the time. He did not want to engage with me at the moment, so he had denied talking about Max and basically had told me to mind my business. And yet, he was engaging with me. I would not let it be, either. "I know you're talking about Max, darling! You can't fool me," I'd say, smiling. And sometimes he would reward me with another word: "Yes."

Nat is always a surprise, sometimes because he shows me that he is just a teenage kid, and not a Disabled Teenager.

This was clear when, another time, I heard him saying, "Pee-iss" and giggling. Could it be . . . ? Yes. Nat was laughing at body parts, just like so many kids do!

Thus I realized that the words at the end of Nat's seemingly senseless phrases were full of meaning. This small glimpse into Nat's mind felt as good to me as any conversation a mother could have with her teenage son.

It is often difficult for me to remember that Nat's own particular development and progress is actually OK. I guess I am scarred in some way since his babyhood, when nothing went as planned. But sometimes his phases parallel Max's so strongly that I get a kind of flash of understanding: They are both teenagers, after all, and they are both leaving the nest, one way or another.

One night during the summer Nat left home, I got a call at eleven P.M. from Max, who had gone off to Vermont for a week with his girlfriend's family. I had put him on a Greyhound bus Monday morning, reaching up to hug his hard, broad shoulders and to kiss his impassive face. It smarted just a bit to let him go, and to see how eager he was for me to leave the bus terminal.

I asked Max to call me when he arrived, but he forgot until late in the evening. I was actually fine about it, but he didn't know that. Even though I had felt some trepidation for him, traveling four hours on his own among strangers, I also felt the excitement he must be feeling, setting out on his first journey alone, to be with his very favorite person.

Max was a little sheepish on the phone at first, knowing he had not done what I had asked him to do. But there was something else that shaped his tone, a roundness, a curl of happiness that I had never before heard from him on the phone, or perhaps had not heard it in a long time. What surprised and touched me even more was the content. He kept offering information, descriptions. He told me how cows were "really disgusting, because they lick their noses and so their faces are always wet with either saliva or snot," and then he laughed. He described the beautiful large house he was staying in, the icy-cold pond, the crazy stars.

When I got off the phone, I felt happy, full. I think it was because for the first time in a long time, Max really wanted to talk to me. What I realized then was that even though things were so different for us these days, we were all still connected. My sixteen-year-old *and* my eighteen-year-old were both moving on from here, but neither one had let me go.

8

Looking toward the Future
Independence and Advocacy

AS NAT GROWS UP, I have had to get used to letting other adults, such as the staff at his residence, take over some of my role. At first it was very difficult for me to trust any new adult that came into Nat's life. It used to fall to Ned and me to make sure Nat was healthy and happy; to make sure that he had a social life, and to get Nat into sports, or into any kind of extracurricular activity. There was so much about Nat that I felt only Ned and I understood: his way of talking, his temper flare-ups, his unusual food preferences (such as eating only the inside of a sandwich, not the bread; or taking the cheese off the pizza and eating only the crust). How would teachers or residential staff learn the subtle signs and figure out if Nat was hurt, or sick?

I used to go through so much frustration with the professionals in Nat's life because, naturally, everyone had a different viewpoint on how to do things. I had to learn to step back, be flexible, and to watch and listen and perhaps learn from others. It was difficult to trust, and then, it was a wondrous thing to learn that Ned and I were not the only ones who could work with—and connect to—Nat. This realization helped us begin a new life focused more on our own happiness and well-being and not only on Nat's.

It took a long time for me to see, again and again, that Nat's teachers were well trained and capable, compassionate and conscientious. They could put more effort into teaching Nat than I could because they were not all tangled up with him emotionally, and they had not been with him day and night for years and years.

Now—at long last—we find ourselves much more able to enjoy Nat's success from the sidelines, cheering him on but allowing others to guide him. This became literally the case when Donnie, Nat's house manager, organized Nat's housemates into a Special Olympics basketball team.

I asked Donnie what that experience had been like for him. It seemed like an ambitious undertaking, to say the least. Donnie confirmed that. Back in the early fall, when he first started coaching the boys and saw how far they had to go, he'd wondered, "Lord, what did I take on?" For one thing, Nat and his housemates do not naturally attend to one another. Nor do they necessarily grasp the basic rules of a game like basketball. So it was up to Donnie to figure out how to teach them everything from watching a teammate's actions, to looking up when someone shouts out your name, to aiming for the basket. "Our kids don't talk to each other, they don't say 'Hey, pass me the ball.' We had to find a way around that," he says. He laughed as he remembered the experience of coaching Nat's team: "I never questioned the kids' hearts. They all played well—to the extent of their abilities. I had one kid who was really happy running up and down the court and giving the other team the ball—that was the extent of his ability. But every time I needed them to run at practice, they did it for me. Every time I needed them to practice shooting the ball, they did it for me."

Donnie described for me some of the steps he took to get his guys to understand the principles of the game: "During practice we would put circles on the floor. Each student would pick a different color circle and put them on different ends of the court. Nat would always pick yellow, so I'd say, "Nat, run a yellow!" and he'd go running up and down the court. "Nat, run a yellow! Nat, run down the court." Sometimes he'd get caught up in his stimming and he didn't care if it was yellow or the court! But, that's something I'm prepared to work with." After months of hard practice and tight routines, the team surpassed all expectations. They ended up winning both games in their tournament. "I was so proud of those guys," said Donnie. "I cried like a baby. I remember Nat, for instance, hadn't been able to hit the basket if it'd been the side of the Empire State Building. I'd give him shot after shot after shot at practice, but nothing would happen. . . . And to see him produce like he did at the State Games, right in front of his parents, I couldn't help but feel proud about that." (Nat ended up making five baskets in the two games.)

I, too, am so proud of Nat, and all he has accomplished over the years, from forming friendships, to living away from home, to working diligently, to controlling his frustrations, to his emergence as a young man contributing positively to the world around him. I never thought we would get to where we are. And we would not have gotten here without finding others, like Donnie, to move us forward.

Before I had children, I could never have believed what motherhood is really like. But in my experience, life forces us to be ready for things even when we're not. We get pregnant, and eventually we go into labor, regardless of where our minds are. One minute you're by yourself, the next, you have a new complicated human being depending on you. Then in the blink of an eye it is time for them to go to school. They have to go and we have to let them. And so we eventually adjust.

I find that my own ability to connect with Nat continues to grow as I gain more and more perspective. Having him live apart from me gives me the time and distance I need to process our relationship, and develop new insights. And as Nat matures, he is more amenable to new experiences, which in turn makes it easier for us to try new things together.

At the end of May, when Nat was nineteen, I learned that his school would be having a prom, for the first time in its history. Terese, Nat's teacher, told me with breathless excitement another wonderful thing: the boys would be getting tuxes! Ever the romantic, I immediately conjured up images of debonair Nat, dressed in crisp white and black. And I wondered: how would he feel, dressed up like that? Would he understand how special it was? I really hoped so.

Terese assured me that as a class they would go over what a prom was and what to expect, so that they would be able to fully appreciate it. The kids would be encouraged to dance together; the school is all-autistic, so the kind of gregarious behavior associated with proms was not something that would come naturally to any of the students. No problem to Terese, however: she would teach them with social stories, which would outline behavior, step-by-step, such as how to ask someone to dance.

The anticipation of the prom made me starry-eyed for a few weeks, and I bragged to everyone I knew that Nat was going to a prom. I wanted the whole world to celebrate the dream with me, the fact that this very disabled boy had come so far. I was also so impressed that his school had evolved to such a capable and humane level that they could offer such a wonderful experience to the kids. Every now and then I checked in with Terese, and then the residence staff, to see how it was going with the prom planning. All was well. The boys would be visited by a tuxedo store at the nearby mall, and they would be fitted. They would also pick out their own colors.

A week before the prom I started to ask Nat all about it, to gauge what he knew about this upcoming event. "Are you going to wear special clothes for the prom, Nat?"

"Yes," he answered.

"What colors are you wearing, Nat?"

"Yelloworange," he said, as if it were one word.

At the time, I thought this answer meant he had chosen a yellow or orange cummerbund and tie. Now, however, I realize that he was telling me what he was wearing at the moment (a yellow T-shirt). Because of his language comprehension difficulties Nat tends to think completely in the present. Sometimes, with his lack of conversational references to the past or future, he seems almost Buddhist in his immersion in the moment.

The morning of the prom, I was so excited. I couldn't wait to take pictures of Nat in his tux. I called the residence to ask what color boutonniere I should get him. But the house manager told me that there were no tuxes. "It didn't work out," she said sorrowfully.

What?! Disappointment shot through my veins like poison. I tried to restrain my emotions, and quickly got off the phone. No tux. Yellow and orange tie? Not going to happen. After all that anticipation, it would just be a regular party. And Nat would be denied one more rite of passage that every other teenager gets.

I was furious. If I had known this would happen, I would have taken him myself to a tuxedo store weeks ago! Just like when Nat was younger, I retreated to my "'No one can really take proper care of Nat but me" stance. My dull, heavy anger traveled slowly up to my brain, but all of a sudden, it sharpened into an idea. I had about four hours before I had to get Nat to the prom. I was damned if he was going there in a tweed jacket and jeans. I was going to get him a tux—*now*.

I started calling every tux place in the Yellow Pages. But it was too early and on a Saturday. I left frantic messages, "Please call back if you can help!" I tried every chain that promised any kind of tux on the market. Nothing was open. No one called back.

Finally, I got through to someone. A soft-spoken man answered the store phone, and I described Nat's size. He reassured me right away that they had what we needed. Ned and I wasted no time and we whisked Nat off in the car.

The store was crammed with black suits, smooth and elegant, on white mannequins. I saw row after row of glossy silk vests with bow ties—even a yellow one, which I hoped Nat wouldn't want, because there was a baby-blue one that would be perfect with his eyes.

The man took in all that was Nat without raising an eyebrow. Good; I could not deal with explaining why my son was tromping through his store, waving his arms and shaking his fist, talking to himself in his own language. But I knew what Nat was feeling, because he was walking and talking so fast, wearing a wide grin and bursting into occasional giggles. Nat was clearly happy about the tux store, and perhaps about the entire prom.

Soon Nat emerged from the dressing room in black jacket, pants, and crisp pleated white shirt. I drew in my breath. He looked utterly beautiful, perfect. This was my son, my boy—but he was such a man! I fell in love with him all over again. How blessed we were!

"Oh," I said, tears in my voice, "you look like a prince." Ned laughed at me because he loves how overly sentimental I get. I blushed and drew out the baby-blue vest, and as I helped Nat button the stiff buttons, I suddenly heard in my head the words from *Sleeping Beauty*, one of Nat's all-time favorite Disney movies. "Why, it's my dream prince," I said, imitating Princess Aurora.

I was trying to be light, but I was too overcome with the

moment. All the different realizations were bursting like fire-works, one after another: Nat, looking so handsome, and princely; the kind, helpful stranger materializing, like a Fairy Godfather, with just the right tuxedo at just the right time; Ned and me, old enough to have a son going to a prom. And also, of course, there was autism, right here, all around us—and yet it made no difference.

Nat went off to his prom, and as soon as he saw his house-mates and teachers, I think he forgot all about us. They applauded his tux and he rewarded them with his wide, glorious smile. Most of the other boys had managed to get tuxes, too. One of his best friends had been named Prom King, and was bouncing around with a red velvet crown on his head. I actually felt a moment's jealousy that it wasn't Nat, but then I thought, "Well, Nat can't have everything!" and laughed at myself. But he did have so much, I realized: he now had two homes and he loved them both.

CONNECTING WITH AUTISTIC ADULTS

I have come to know many ASD adults on Yahoo groups and blogs on the Internet, and I have learned so much from them, which only helps my interactions with Nat by giving me greater understanding and empathy into autistic experiences. I recently heard from a nineteen-year-old man with Asperger's, Cale from Long Island, New York, who also has a brother with classic autism. Cale had a lot to say about the need to study further the genes tied to autism: "Not so that there can be a purge of autistic fetuses, but rather so that parents can know earlier about their child's neurological condition, and thus bypass the years of confusion and frustration that separate the onset of symptoms and the actual diagnosis."

He also mentioned the need to improve the tools for helping autistics communicate with the world. Cale would start by strengthening the PECS (Picture Exchange Communication System) program, which enables nonverbal people to communicate by choosing a labeled picture among a large selection of picture cards, and by exploring the potential of communication-facilitation devices—anything that allows autistics to communicate in the way they are able, and not only have to rely on verbal speech.

One thing that has made a lasting impression on me is what ASD adults have to say about the biases they experience regarding communication. Neurotypical society has a strong bias toward verbal communication. Many autistic adults on my e-mail list are either nonverbal—they type on their computers instead—or they are very uncomfortable with speaking (processing and accessing words verbally rapidly is challenging for them). These ASD adults discuss what it is like for them when they have to speak; the difficulty of paying attention to the correct, intended conversation thread; the necessity of ignoring distracting noises; the discomfort of making eye contact—all so challenging for them—and then to have many people in the world view them as inferior people when they cannot manage these skills.

These discussions are both eye-opening and poignant, and I wonder if it feels that way for Nat. My views on what should be considered "normal" or "high-functioning" have changed considerably since coming to know some autistic adults. You don't have to be verbal—or typically wired—to be a full person.

The ASD adult blogs and e-mail lists provide a very helpful perspective to parents, not only in terms of having greater empathy for the atypically developing person, for they can also give us hope. When you meet so many autistic adults, with such varying degrees of autism, and then come to know them as people, you realize all the potential in human beings—including your own child's. You see that so much is possible for all of us in today's world, and especially for people with autism as a result of all the helpful communication technology, inclusive public education, and increasing societal efforts toward tolerance. Understanding all of this firsthand can give us a sense of wonder and hope—and what can be more important than that in our quest to be happy and at peace with our lives?

Connecting with Autistic Adults Online

- Check out the Autistic Self Advocacy Network (ASAN) autisticadvocacy.org/, an advocacy organization run by and for autistics, providing support, resources, and action points for improving the quality of life for those with ASDs. When our children are old enough, perhaps they can check out this Web site themselves.

- Go to youtube.com and search for "In My Language" by Amanda Baggs. This video offers a very different kind of perspective about autism and communication, emphasizing the biases that verbal people have toward the nonverbal by showing you a nonverbal woman who communicates very effectively. On the video, she engages in self-stimulatory behavior (waving things back and forth, singing in a monotonous voice, rocking) and then uses a voice simulation program to explain what her behaviors mean to her. She also points out the biases of our society in terms of what we view as "disabled" when perhaps what we are viewing is only "different." It presents another useful way for parents to understand autism and maybe help their kids live a life of their own.

- Search on the Web for "Don't Mourn for Us" by Jim Sinclair. This piece will give you accurate and moving insights into being differently wired.

- You can find a collection of autism blogs, by autistics and nonautistics, by going to autism-hub.co.uk. It gives a diverse spectrum of views that are informative, honest, sometimes devastating, and often moving.

FOSTERING INDEPENDENCE

Peter Gerhardt, president for the Organization for Autism Research (OAR), is another professional I have come to know who like Donnie conveys the feeling of hope and has a "can do" attitude that is contagious. OAR is researching how to maximize the skills of teens and adults on the spectrum to get them out of the house and into the community and the workplace.

In terms of our own happiness as parents, what could be a better achievement than our children's independence and competence in the outside world? Peter also has a private practice consulting with families, employers, and school systems to help people on the spectrum learn to live independently. He has had tremendous success helping even those considered "unemployable" to land and keep jobs. "Everybody can learn, but we all need sufficient practice before we are proficient at any task."

Peter always begins his assessment of his clients by asking the following questions, and he advises parents to do the same:

1. What skills would benefit you?

2. How do we teach them to you?

3. How do you maintain those skills?

To Peter, the goal is to help people acquire independent living skills, whether it's the ability to work in a restaurant or simply first being able to order a meal on one's own in a restaurant. If we parents keep our eye on the ultimate goals and don't lose sight of them, we can help our children progress toward independence, which is part of the picture of our own happiness. "The goal is to fade out subsidized supports," Peter says. But he is quick to add that we still need to have "natural supports" for autistics in the workplace and in the community—regular folks who are sympathetic and ready to help.

How do you go about fostering natural supports for your child? "If I want to teach grocery shopping," says Peter, "I use the supermarket the parents go to. I figure out where is the friendly cashier, when is he or she on?" He introduces his client to this friendly clerk, keeping it simple, and trying to enlist her support. "Ninety percent of the community people are welcoming and want to help. The other ten percent, well . . . ." Autism parents know all about the other 10 percent unfortunately. The good news is, most of the time things are fairly smooth with the outside world. People are relatively understanding, they try to help, and forays into the community usually end successfully. "Build on the positive experiences," Peter advises. "Look for a pattern, make your foray into the community as positive an experience as possible." For example, he works to build these experiences by repeating the same activity a few times, such as having the child purchase a hamburger or pick up dry cleaning while the parent waits in the car right outside. "We do that for three days, and then add on to it."

Peter's focused and individualized approach has helped hundreds of autistic clients be successful in the workplace. Even the "higher functioning" student can learn from this approach. Functional education is a must for people on the spectrum. "But some parents feel that the word *functional* somehow means giving up on their child academically," says Peter. "Life skills allow you to use your academic skills. Even the kid who is going to college needs to learn the social nice-ties of small talk, how to dress for an interview, and so forth. Autism parents often want to focus only on the academics, but it is not an either/or situation."

Parents also need be optimistic, do pragmatic planning, and allow themselves to dream and look ahead to the future, using their intuition about what's best and possible for the child. "Autism families spend so much time thinking about what they can't do," Peter says. "Ask yourself, 'What's the worst thing that can happen?' Have a plan for that, but don't let it stop you. We're so conditioned to think that when we're out in the community things have to be perfect." But we don't have to be perfect, and neither do our kids, though we do need to plan out what we're going to do if things don't go well.

For more information on getting your child ready to live independently, take a look at the *Transition Guide* pub-lished by the Organization for Autism Research on their Web site, spectrumtrainingsystemsinc.com/petergerhardt.html. Also check out Paul Wehman's book, *Life beyond the Class-room: Transition Strategies for Young People with Disabilities.*

TURNING CHALLENGE INTO ADVOCACY

Jane, a kindred spirit in Milwaukee, is way ahead of me. Her son, Chris, is thirty-three. "My son has been working at Barnes and Noble and living in an adult family home in the community for eleven years," she wrote me. "I *still* suffer from separation anxiety and miss him every day (even though I do see him every weekend). I can tell you that I still do not know if this is the course he would have chosen for himself. He does not verbally indicate whether he is happy or not (he has limited speech). We judge his well-being via his behavior." This has always been our modus operandi with Nat, who so often cannot or does not express what is going on inside.

Jane impressed me with her positive attitude and her ability to meet difficulties head-on, despite the challenges of being a single mother. "I was divorced when Chris was six or seven years old," she told me. "I really felt alone. I just wanted to take care of my son and daughter. We all moved to Akron, Ohio, because I had a stepsister there. It was great because we had family; we had supports."

The support of her stepsister enabled Jane to go back to school and earn a degree that would help her get a good job. After she finished her education, the three of them moved back to Milwaukee and lived with Jane's parents while Jane looked for a job. Jane feels she was so lucky to have been able to do that, as opposed to feeling discouraged about moving in with her parents. "Those were the happiest days of Chris's life," Jane said. Even now, twenty-six years later, he points in the direction of her parents' old house when they pass their old neighborhood. It is Jane's dream to buy her parents' former home so that Chris can live in it again.

Jane's strong sense of what is important and her ability to stick with that has convinced her that advocacy is the key to an autism family's happiness: advocacy for the child and for the parent. "I want more for him," she said simply. "I want to build a better world for him while he's alive." Doing that is a tall order, but Jane has learned that facing the obstacles that come up gives her such a feeling of accomplishment. "You have to stay on top of all the tasks related to supporting Chris as an adult in the world. It never ends. But it's the challenge of it all that interests me," she said. "If you're negative, all the work you've accomplished will cave in. It is just that simple. Chris can sense my attitude. It affects him in so many ways." And being negative will affect you, the parent, as well.

Jane also discovered the value of finding trustworthy people who understand her child. One such person helped Jane's son Chris to get the job he has had for eleven years at Barnes & Noble. "Chris had a job at a public library," says Jane. "There was a woman there who knew how to connect with him. When this woman left the library to work at Barnes and Nobel herself, she took Chris with her." Since then, she has acted as a job coach and sometimes serves as a liaison between Chris and the customers. But it is Chris's ability to internalize the layout of the bookstore that has made him the cherished employee he is today. "He knows just about where every book is in the store," says Jane. "He helps customers. He walks them to where their book is."

It is clear that much of Jane's happiness and sense of fulfillment comes from her relationship with Chris, both in helping him and in enjoying him. "Chris makes me happy just being with him," she says. But she wants more for him than just happiness. "I work with agencies that work with Chris. I try to educate them. I know that I can make a difference."

Michael Goldberg, a Massachusetts autism dad and the editor of *The Autism Bulletin,* a blog, autismbulletin.blog spot.com, that keeps track of changes in autism policies nationwide, says, "Make the effort to educate yourself and become aware. Then spread that awareness in your own style, and don't stop." Parents, families, and organizations big and small are what create the changes in policies that affect the autistic people in their lives. Michael points to the success of organizations such as Easter Seals, Autism Speaks, and the Autism Society of America, which have recently become a visible part of the national-issues landscape, powerfully influencing the passage of such federal legislation as the Combating Autism Act of 2007.

But just as important are the smaller advocacy groups. "In a number of states around the country there are parents and other advocates who are getting together with their state legislators," says Michael. "These autism advocates have established task forces to survey the existing services, what health insurance covers, and so forth, and they produce reports that eventually go before the legislature and the governor." According to Michael, Texas and South Carolina have already produced landmark legislation ordering health care insurers to cover certain autism therapies such as speech and occupational therapy, and other states are following.

There are supports and services out there, but as Jane would say, "it is slim pickings." In order for autistic people—and just as important, their families—to have lives worth living, much more needs to happen. "I compare this to the civil rights movement," says Michael. "The autism quality-of-life movement needs to build up enough momentum for the bills to pass." The only way for this to happen is through our own efforts. Jane summed it up best: "Get politically involved. Talk to your legislators. Talk to as many people as you can. Find out what your options are. We need more voices. My voice is faint, because my son was diagnosed before the steep rise in autism, and that is frustrating. But the younger parents have a louder voice. There's power in numbers."

Feeling our power makes us feel alive. We need to feel our own vitality and strength as autism parents and as individuals in our own right. It is by realizing our own energy and potential that we can create a balanced and happy life for our families and, of course, for ourselves.

Get Involved in Advocacy Efforts

- Look at the Easter Seals Web site, which gives you a breakdown, state-by-state, of the autism legislation in process (easterseals.com). Find out who your state and federal representatives are and send letters, make phone calls. Government officials need proof of constituent support; they can use our letters to help persuade their colleagues.

- The ARC of the United States also lists important legislation and has a weekly newsletter, Capitol Insider, at thearc.org/NetCommunity/Page.aspx?pid=420. You can also sign up to get e-mail reminders of when to contact your representatives. Go to capwiz.com/thearc/mlm/signup/.

- Some local organizations (such as community ARCs or regional autism support centers) conduct lobbying workshops that teach parents how to meet with their legislators.

- Grassroots action is always necessary. Across the country, parent advisory councils (PACs) exist in one form or another, to help educate special-needs parents. Check out the National Parent Teacher Association Web site (pta.org) to find out what is going on by searching the word "disability."

- Find out what is happening in your local school system. Sitting down regularly with the cochairs of your PAC and the school administration is one of the most important ways to improve conditions for special-needs families. The following organization is a great model: brooklinesepac.org/index.php/events/.

- Another way to influence opportunities for your child in your own town is to get your Parks and Recreation Department to expand their offerings for special-needs kids. Brookline Quest is an organization in my town that my friend Dyanne and several others founded that organizes social outings for Nat and his friends every other Friday night, leaving Friday nights free for the parents to have some fun on their own! (See brook linequest.org/.) Similarly, Alternative Leisure (alctrips .com/) offers social activities and all-around fun for teens and adults with special needs. If there's no program like this near you, consider starting your own!

Concluding Thoughts

*If I ever go looking for my heart's desire
again, I won't look any farther than my
own backyard.*

—Dorothy, in *The Wizard of Oz*

RECENTLY WE DECIDED to take a trip to New York City
with just Max and Ben, leaving Nat in his residence at school
for the weekend. We needed some special time together, free
to do anything we wanted, and Ned and I needed a chance
to focus all of our attention on Max and Ben. I also wanted
them to experience New York without any fears or distrac-
tions. (Unfortunately, bringing Nat along sometimes meant
just that to me and to them: fear and distraction.)

The week before our trip, I took Nat back to school Saturday afternoon, knowing that we would not be seeing him the
following weekend (thus far, our routine had been to bring
him home Friday night and return him to school on Saturday afternoon). I told Nat about the change of routine for the
coming week so that he would not expect to come home that

Friday. His mood was fine; he went right back into the classroom, right into his school routine, and I sat in a chair there to watch him for a few minutes before going back home.

As I drove home, my mood started to drop. I put in a load of laundry and unloaded groceries. When I was finished, I put on some music, an old song with a lovely melody. But the lyrics were so sad: "So soon, so soon, the day is gone." A flood of emotion just burst out of me, sudden and sharp.

I knew what had brought it on: my ever-present guilt, my regrets about Nat. Too soon. It was all too soon. Even though I knew that our family was doing so well, feeling so light, *without Nat* (it rips me up even now to write that), still I hated that fact. I wanted him back. I wanted all of this to go away, his move-out, his weeklong absences. Even our progress did not matter to me in that moment. I wanted my son with me, and that's all there was to it.

But I knew that could not happen, should not happen. Nat's progress mattered. Our family's newfound ease and lightness and flexibility mattered. Still, a whirlpool of grief sucked me downward, and I was swirling in that void once again, torn between what Nat needed and what I wanted.

Evil, self-destructive thoughts kept circling around my head like vultures: once again I'd let him go because others said I should. I had given up. I sank down into a dining room chair and could not stop crying like a little kid—shaky, breathless sobs, wet face pressed to the table. The simple fact was that Nat was not coming home this week because we were going to New York without him. We were going to have fun without him. How could I allow that?

Even while I was submerged in this emotional swamp, a tiny bubble of reason was surfacing. I knew I couldn't just allow myself to be this miserable; at least, not for long. I still had my routines and responsibilities. My children. Ned. My students, my friends, my writing. I also have myself, my own life's happiness, to nurture as well.

I called Ned on the phone, but he was not around. But somewhere in my clouded head I knew I had to find someone else to help me, because this felt really bad.

It was one of those moments of quiet distance, when we can stop and step outside of what is happening to us. That capacity to step back and reflect seems key to our survival. And in this way I began to pull myself up.

I called my therapist, and she actually answered the phone (how often does that happen? Sometimes things happen just right.). She listened and quickly got a handle on what was going on.

"I'm trying to tease it all apart," I told her.

She said, "You know, sometimes it's really therapeutic to be with difficult emotions, to untangle them and figure it all out. But other times it's actually better to pull back from them and simply reconnect with your daily activities."

I considered this, while searching for a tissue to staunch the flow from my eyes and nose.

"Is there something you could do, some task that needs to get done, that could maybe take you out of the house for a little while?"

I thought of the large sheath of final exams from my students' last class. "Well, I have some papers to grade," I said.

"So why not go to a cafe or something," she said, "some-place where you will be among people—not to talk to them but just be around people in general and in that way recon-nect with other sides of yourself?"

I agreed this might be a good idea, and after I hung up, I set about getting my papers ready. A little while later I was sitting at a table at Starbucks, by a window that looked out onto a busy street. I was smiling at something a student of mine had written on his final exam while I sipped an extra-sweet coffee. A sultry rendition of "Baby, It's Cold Outside" was playing, and even though it seemed corny, and a little too early for Christmas music, I started daydreaming about the upcoming Christmas vacation, when we'd be watching movies as a family, baking gingerbread with Nat (probably because I could smell this in the air in the store).

I looked out at everyone around me, and realized I felt like a person again, a grown-up, sitting there full of purpose and daydreams of the future, no longer miserable about my oldest son, who was off and living his own life.

I considered what had happened a little while ago, back home. What if I had listened to something like this bouncy song, instead of that tragic song? Had I done this to myself? Maybe I needed to have a good cry, to reconnect my heart to Nat. Whatever it was about, those raw moments had passed, and now I felt cleaned out and fresh.

I don't know the answer to all of this, but I do know that we all end up doing what we have to do, and sometimes it's not that pretty. Only rarely can we get to a spa somewhere and have someone massage away our troubles. Even then, we still always have to come back to our lives. So, most of the time, we have to take care of ourselves somehow, then and there, even in the middle of a child's tantrum. Somehow we hold on to sanity, maybe when a lifeline-person takes our kid for an hour and we go out on a bike ride or a drive. Sometimes we lock ourselves in the bathroom and cry, and then we come out and find a loved one to hug. Sometimes we leave the house for a brief walk. Sometimes we share a bubble of time with our spouse, a flirtatious text message or a joke about our kids. Sometimes we lose ourselves in dance, or song, or books, or a ride on a Harley.

Perhaps we just need to get ourselves to a little coffee shop where there are good smells in the air, to find a small, quiet moment in which to step away from it all. I think that's the secret: that there is no secret, there is no magic to feeling joy and contentment in our difficult lives. There is only the gift of perspective, the embrace of relationships, the safety of our favorite places, the comfort of the things we find beautiful, and the endless ways we can find pleasure, big and small.

And of course, there is something just as important as all of that: ourselves. We don't have to give that up for anything or anyone. We do not have to trade our selves for our children, or our happiness for our children's happiness. Even something as confounding and difficult as autism in the family is not the end of a happy life. Struggle, grief, and disappointment still do not change the fact that we deserve to be happy. But it starts right here, with ourselves, in our own backyard, affirming our own importance both in our family *and* in our life. Once we understand that, we will get there, and it will all be OK.

Epilogue

RECENTLY, in a particularly upbeat moment, it struck me that I could imagine my life with Nat like a kind of game. I envision it looking a lot like Candyland, Nat's all-time favorite game. In my game, "Autismland," you wander into various areas of the board and you go through a series of steps forward and steps backward. The places you land in are called things like "Diagnosis Den" or "Team Meeting Maze," where you lose a turn as you deal with things such as evaluations or the need to learn new jargon.

Sometimes you land on a square where you might go a few steps forward because your child has acquired a less severe diagnosis than in the past. But you may also end up on a square that reads, "Your child is too high-functioning for services, go back three spaces." There are areas such as "Medication Morass," where you lose a turn as you try to get your child's medication and dosage right; nearby is the "Mainstream Classroom Castle," which rests on clouds. But watch out because a few steps later, you might land on the "Residential Placement" square. There is also a fork in the path that sends you into the "Alternative Therapy Abyss," where you lose time, money, and energy. And yet, the other side of the fork might take you to "Alternative Therapy Alley," where you go ahead a few spaces because your child's skills are improving due to some new approach you've tried.

The game keeps going for a while because there are so many setbacks, so many tricky areas to navigate. Many who play this game believe that the winner is the one whose child is cured. But that's not the case.

There's a lot of truth to this metaphor, bizarre though it may be—especially the fact that you feel lost for so long when you are dealing with autism. As an autism parent, you see your child progress, regress, and progress again. When your child does well, you feel proud, as if maybe you did something right. And when your kid is struggling, you feel responsible, as if you failed. You lose a lot of sleep and you wonder how this will end.

Then one day, maybe gradually, or maybe in a flash, you realize that you are no longer asking that question. Though nothing has changed outwardly in your situation, you are no longer feeling mired in some dead-end place. Something inside you has shifted, lightened. When you look at your child, you no longer see a mass of problems, a broken thing to be fixed; you see your kid, just your kid. You realize you just want to have some fun with him. Or maybe you want to think about something else altogether. Or be with your spouse. Whatever you do, you realize it's going to be OK. It's just your life, warts, autism, and all. And you can't wait to start living it to its fullest.

You have just won the game.

Resources

Important, Honest Books That Illustrate Acceptance

Beck, Martha. *Expecting Adam*. New York: Penguin Group, 2001.

———. *The Joy Diet*. New York: Random House, 2003.

Greenfeld, Karl Taro. *Boy Alone*. New York: HarperCollins, 2009.

Haddon, Marc. *The Curious Incident of the Dog in the Night-Time*. New York: Doubleday, 2003.

Isaacson, Rupert. *Horse Boy*. New York: Little, Brown, 1999.

Parish, Robert. *Embracing Autism*. Hoboken, N.J.: Jossey-Bass, 2008.

Robison, John Elder. *Look Me in the Eyes*. New York: Crown, 2007.

Senator, Susan. *Making Peace with Autism*. Boston: Trumpeter Books, 2005.

Movies about Difference (Not Only Autism)

Gillespie, Craig. *Lars and the Real Girl*. MGM, 2007.

Hall, Elaine, et al. *Autism, the Musical*. Docurama Films, 2008.

McCarthy, Thomas. *The Station Agent*. Miramax, 2003.

Trachtman, Ilana. *Praying with Lior*. First Run Features, 2009.

Index

"10 Steps to Feeling Good Naked"
(*O* magazine), 94
acceptance of child with autism, 9,
19–22, 41–42, 50–55
advocacy
Autism Society of America (ASA),
19, 44
Autism Speaks, 178; autism walks, 136
Autistic Self-Advocacy Network
(ASAN), 21, 171
Brookline Quest, 180
Combating Autism Act of 2007, 178
Easter Seals, 178–79
Parent Advisory Councils (PAC), 180
Parks and Recreation, 180–81
on state level, 178
See also under ARC, The
Alastair from Cape Town, South Africa,
narrative of, 87–88, 94, 105
Alice from Texas, narrative of, 69, 90–91
American Academy of Pediatrics, 12
Amy from Washington, narrative of, 67,
88, 93, 94, 122–23
Alternative Leisure Company. *See
under* recreational activities
antidepressants. *See under* medication
Applied Behavior Analysis (ABA), 45,
48, 63, 69, 116, 134
ARC, The (formerly Association of
Retarded Citizens), 17, 179–80
lobbying workshops, 180
Ariel, Cindy, 114
Asperger's Syndrome, 13, 31, 130, 153, 169
Ativan. *See under* medication
au pair. *See under* child care
Autism and the God Connection (Stillman), 21
autism, negative perceptions of, 7–8
coping with, 16–19
freeing from, 19–22
See also acceptance of child with
autism; disability baggage
Autism Bulletin, The. See under blogs

autism divide. *See under*
biomedical and neurodiversity,
conflict between
Autism Project, 48
See also Buie, Tim
Autistic Self Advocacy Network. *See
under* advocacy
Autism Society of America (ASA). *See
under* advocacy
Autism Speaks. *See under* advocacy
autism spectrum
ambiguity of, 28–30
burden of broadness, 28–30, 31–35
high functioning, 28
low functioning, 28
See also Pervasive Developmental
Disorder, Not Otherwise Specified (PDD-NOS)
Autism Spectrum Disorder (ASD), 32
adults with, 169–72
autism walks. *See* advocacy: Autism
Speaks
Autism's False Prophets (Offit), 46
aversive therapies. *See under* therapies

Baggs, Amanda. *See* "In My Language"
baking with your child, 67–68, 186
behavior management, 2, 27
belly dance. *See under* self-care
Beth from Texas, narrative of, 87
betta fish, caring for. *See under* self-care
Bettelheim, Bruno (and "refrigerator
mother"), 7
biomedical and neurodiversity, conflict
between, 41–46
biomedical treatment or intervention,
20, 31, 35–40, 48
blogs, 29, 91, 105
Autism Bulletin, The, 178
and connecting with autistic adults,
169, 171, 172
opinionated, 17, 18, 42–43
writing, 21–22, 138, 139, 152

About the Author

SUSAN SENATOR is the mother of three boys, the oldest of whom has autism. A writer, speaker, and advocate for children and the disabled, she is the author of *Making Peace with Autism: One Family's Story of Struggle, Discovery, and Unexpected Gifts.*

Susan's writing on autism has appeared in the *New York Times*, the *Washington Post*, the *Boston Globe, Education Week, Teacher* magazine, and *Exceptional Parent* magazine. She has also been featured on the *Today* show, CNN, NPR, and MSNBC. In 2006, in recognition of her writing about autism and the Special Olympics, she was invited to the White House.

For more information, autism resources, or to read her blog, visit susansenator.com.